Praise for

Best Preschool for Your Child

"This well-organized, comprehensive book will help parents navigate the world of preschool admissions. Its practical, clear advice breaks down this sometimes overwhelming process and gives parents helpful guidance."

—Nancy Schulman and Ellen Birnbaum,
authors of *Practical Wisdom for Parents: Raising Self-Confident Children in the Preschool Years* and
directors of the 92nd Street Y Nursery School

"I highly recommend this book—it's the most useful tool out there for families about to embark on the search for a preschool! Not only does it provide sound advice on how to navigate through the admissions process, it's also filled with useful information on helping your child get ready for this new experience, from handling separation anxiety to packing lunch and snacks for your preschooler."

—Helen Cohen, director, Frances
Jacobson Early Childhood Center

"All families who are beginning the search for a preschool need to read this book. It is well organized, approachable, and takes a well thought out approach to the preschool selection process."

—Aimee Giles, director of admission,
Children's Day School

"*How to Choose the Best Preschool for Your Child* is a gift to every parent starting the preschool search. It offers clear and detailed advice on every aspect of the search, so that parents can make an informed decision for their child."

—Irene Byrne, MA, author of *Preschools by the Bay* and executive director of the Phoebe Hearst Preschool

"Any parent questioning where and when to send their child to nursery school should definitely buy this book! It gives invaluable insight on finding and getting into the right preschool for your child."

—Victoria Goldman, author of *The Manhattan Directory of Private Nursery Schools*

"*How to Choose the Best Preschool for Your Child* is a must-read for any parent looking for a preschool. Jenifer Wana's book offers practical, step-by-step advice to help parents find a program that fits their child and family's needs."

—Lee Ann Slaton, MS, former Parents Place education coordinator for over twenty years

"This guide reveals everything you need to know to choose a great preschool. Wana takes what can be a stressful and overwhelming task and transforms it into a simple process any parent can successfully navigate."

—Bill Jackson, president and founder, GreatSchools

HOW TO CHOOSE
THE BEST PRESCHOOL
FOR YOUR CHILD

The Ultimate Guide to
Finding, Getting Into, and
Preparing for Nursery School

JENIFER WANA

Copyright © 2010 by Jenifer Wana
Cover and internal design © 2010 by Sourcebooks, Inc.
Cover design by Jane Archer (www.psbella.com)
Cover images © Beau Lark/Jupiter Images

Published by Sourcebooks, Inc.
P.O. Box 4410, Naperville, Illinois 60567-4410
(630) 961-3900
Fax: (630) 961-2168
www.sourcebooks.com

Library of Congress Cataloging-in-Publication Data

Wana, Jenifer.
  How to choose the best preschool for your child : the ultimate guide to finding, getting into, and preparing for nursery school / by Jenifer Wana.
     p. cm.
  1. Education, Preschool—United States. 2. Nursery schools—United States. 3. Education, Preschool—Parent participation—United States. 4. School choice—United States. 5. Readiness for school—United States. I. Title.
  LB1140.23.W36 2010
  372.210973—dc22
                                2010002995

Printed and bound in the United States of America.

I want to dedicate this book to my husband, Kevin, and our children, Josh and Ruby, whose smiles and laughter inspire me every day.

Contents

Acknowledgments

FIRST, THANKS TO MY HUSBAND, Kevin, for his unwavering encouragement and support since the moment I came up with the idea for this book. I am truly grateful for his never-ending belief in my ability to complete this project. Thanks to my son, Josh, for being a good boy while I worked, and my daughter, Ruby, for sleeping well during the night.

I also want to express my sincere thanks to the following people and organizations:

The preschool directors, admissions professionals, and other experts who shared tips and insights, including Aimee Giles, Diane Larrabee, Nancy Schulman, Ellen Birnbaum, Gretchen Ott, Bea Wilderman, Lysa Farrell, Arthur Anchipolovsky, and Jessica Salinas.

The National Association for the Education of Young Children, the National Association of Child Care Resource & Referral Agencies, and Amy Korytowski Matsui from the National Women's Law Center for reviewing portions of the manuscript.

My friends who read the manuscript and provided valuable

feedback, including Karen Cho, Jieun Choe, Sabrina Moyle, Fermina Phillips, Karen Lee, Karen Shea, and Amy Schigelone; family and friends who provided their assistance and helpful suggestions along the way, including my siblings John, Julie, and Joe Wana, Matthew Chang, Monica Gonzales, Julia Coblentz, Adoria Lim, Nelson Wang, Audrey Gerber, Brigitte Brady-Harris, Andy Sareyan, Cam Chan, and Amy Eschliman.

My parents, Linda and Sunt Wana, and my in-laws, Margarita and Ching-Kuo Chen, for their support and baby-sitting help.

Lisa Jones and Marcia Santore for their terrific editing skills.

Stephanie Kip Rostan, my agent, who believed in the book's potential from the very beginning and found it the perfect home; Shana Drehs, my editor, whose dream and enthusiasm for this project helped turn my vision into a reality.

Lastly, all the parents who shared their experiences and advice for finding and applying to preschool with me—I couldn't have written this book without you.

Introduction

THIS IS THE BOOK I wanted to read when I started looking for a preschool for my son, Josh. Unfortunately, it hadn't been written yet.

Like any parents, my husband and I wanted to find the best place for our son—a preschool that would nurture him, teach him, and be a good fit for our family. But I quickly learned that this would not be as easy as it seemed. I was overwhelmed by the options—when I was growing up, kids just went to the nursery school closest to home, if they went at all. I didn't know where to begin to find the best preschools in my neighborhood or what characteristics defined a high-quality program. Terms like *Montessori, child centered,* and *co-op* were foreign to me. School tours gave me a clearer picture of what each school was like, but I wasn't sure what I should be on the lookout for or what questions I should ask to see if it was the right place for us.

What I also discovered about the preschool process was that there is no process. Unlike college or graduate school, there are no standard time lines or admissions procedures that all nursery schools follow—and very few resources to help parents navigate the process. So I went to preschool fairs, attended seminars and panel discussions, read books and articles, and had countless conversations with other parents who had been through the process. I pored over school websites and brochures, toured schools, and filled out endless applications. For a few programs, I brought Josh in to be observed at "playdates" and wrote essays describing his strengths and challenges.

In the end, we were fortunate, and Josh was accepted to our first-choice school—even though, as we learned later, there were over two hundred applications for thirty spots (most of which went to siblings of students already at the school).

After helping countless other parents navigate their preschool search on the basis of my experience, my research, and the advice I'd received, I decided to pull all of the information together into a book to benefit other parents of soon-to-be preschoolers. I hope to demystify the process for those who don't have access to all the mommy lore from knowledgeable friends and family.

Whether the preschools in your town enroll every child that signs up or are so competitive that they can accept only a few applicants each year, this book will give you the tools you need to find, research, and choose the best programs for your child. You will learn about the different types of preschool philosophies and know how to put your best foot forward when applying to selective schools that can't admit every applicant. This book will also give you practical advice on how to help your child prepare for his or her first preschool experience and have a great first day.

Preschool is the first step in your child's educational journey. I hope that with this book as your guide, you'll be able to find the school that works best for your family, and you will start your child on a lifelong adventure of learning and discovery.

CHAPTER 1

Preschool Primer

PRESCHOOL IS A BIG MILESTONE in your child's life—and in yours. She'll be taking her first step toward independence and into the larger world, away from the security of home and family. Even if she's already in day care, preschool will be her first formal school experience. In either scenario, beginning preschool will be a major transition for everyone in the family.

Early childhood experts say that attending a high-quality preschool program helps to promote children's social and emotional development and prepare them for kindergarten and beyond. Studies have shown that children who attended high-quality early education programs are more likely to have better test scores and grades, go to college, and have better-paying jobs. However, finding the right program for your child can take some preparation and planning. In addition to finding preschools in your area, you'll want to understand their educational approaches, evaluate the differences between programs, and spend time visiting the schools to determine which ones you want to apply to. Then you must figure out each preschool's application procedure, which can be a fairly complicated process because each school has its own system. This can all leave you feeling a bit overwhelmed, especially if you live in an area where it seems like there aren't enough preschool spots to go around.

Your town may have plenty of preschool options. In that case, you may be able to call one close to your home and sign your child up the week before school starts. When I was growing up, most mothers stayed at home with their children and kids played in the yard until they started kindergarten. Kids who did go to nursery school went for a few hours a week at a local church or community center. Mom could stop by and chat with the director, fill out a simple form, choose morning or afternoon, and that was it.

That scenario isn't as common as it once was. Nowadays, there are more two-career and single-parent families, so there is an increased need for the high-quality child care that preschool offers. Nursery school is no longer considered just a nice option or a way to give Mom a break. And as the academic and social benefits of early childhood education become better known, more parents are sending their kids to preschool. Enrollment in early childhood education programs (public and private) has grown from 4 million children in 1970 to more than 6 million today.

As more parents come to understand the benefits of early education, there is also a greater importance placed on which particular preschool their children attend. For new parents who don't know much about preschool in general or about what makes for a high-quality program, it's only natural that they want their child to go to a preschool with a reputation as one of the best in town. It's important to realize, however, that a school's reputation as the "best" or most popular, as having the longest waiting list, or as being the hardest to get into doesn't necessarily mean it's the best for your child. Most parents would probably agree that it's worth the extra research to find preschools that might be a better match. But for many people, it's not clear how or where to begin.

If this whole issue leaves you feeling confused and a little overwhelmed, you're in good company—that's the reaction most parents have. But don't worry, this book will help you navigate the process and find a school that is right for your child. This first chapter will cover the basics.

WHAT IS PRESCHOOL?

The term *preschool* generally refers to the one to three years of schooling before kindergarten. Most preschool programs are for kids between the ages of three and five years old, though some enroll children as early as the age of two. The terms *preschool, nursery school,* and *pre-K* (or *prekindergarten*) are often used interchangeably. You may also hear terms such as *day care, child care center, toddler program, transitional kindergarten,* or *junior kindergarten* in reference to preschool.

Child Care Centers

Whereas preschools typically enroll children between approximately two and a half and five years old, child care (or daycare) centers are designed to provide child care for working parents for children ranging from infants up to preschool age or older. Some preschool programs are housed within child care centers. Once kids turn two or three, if the center places them in a class with other preschool-age kids and there's a teacher who follows a curriculum with structured learning activities, then that is generally considered preschool. Chapter 5 will tell you more about day care as a preschool option and how to determine whether it's right for your situation.

Toddler Program

A toddler program (or parent-toddler program) is offered by some preschools for the diaper set. Some programs will accept toddlers as young as nine or twelve months old and others eighteen months. The purpose of such programs is to introduce the fundamentals of what preschool is all about. Kids get to play with (or next to) one another, explore art and craft materials, enjoy music, and hear stories. Depending on the program, a parent may or may not be required to participate in the class. There is less structure in these programs than in preschool, but the day usually begins and ends with a group circle time. Some toddler programs follow the same half-day or full-day schedule as preschool classes, but others meet only once or twice a week for an hour or two. A toddler program is a great way to provide fun, stimulating activities for your little one. It's also a good way to get to know a school and let the school get to know you. Many preschools also give preference for spots in the preschool class to children who are enrolled in their toddler program.

Pre-K

Many people use the words *pre-K* or *prekindergarten* as another term for preschool, but pre-K also refers to a one-year program geared toward four-year-olds who will enter kindergarten the following year. Pre-K programs are often attached to an elementary school but may also be part of a preschool. Their purpose is to teach kids the skills they will need to succeed in kindergarten to help ease that transition. These types of pre-K classes provide more routine and structured time (e.g., circle time is followed by snack time, then outdoor play) and more pre-reading and pre-math activities than a typical preschool.

Transitional Kindergarten

Another type of pre-K program is known as transitional kindergarten or junior kindergarten. These classes are for kids who are almost five years old and just miss the kindergarten cutoff age but are ready to move on from preschool and for those who are old enough to enter kindergarten but need an extra year to develop socially and emotionally. Transitional kindergarten serves as a half step between preschool and kindergarten. The curriculum is more structured like a kindergarten class but with a slower pace and more playtime. Some children really benefit from the extra time to grow and mature. For more information, see "Should We Delay Kindergarten?" in chapter 3.

DO I HAVE TO SEND MY CHILD TO PRESCHOOL?

By no means do you have to send your child to preschool. Preschool is not mandatory in the United States, as most states don't require children to start formal schooling until the age of six or seven. Some parents choose to keep their kids at home until kindergarten to spend more time together, for financial reasons, or to homeschool their preschooler and have more control over how and what their children are taught.

WHAT ARE THE BENEFITS OF PRESCHOOL?

There are many benefits to enrolling a child in a formal preschool program, though every family has its own reasons. The following sections go over some of the benefits to children and parents.

Stimulation

Some parents sense that their child is ready to explore the world beyond their own home. Especially if she doesn't have siblings or friends she sees every day, she may seem bored at home or spend too much time in front of the television. Is she eager to learn new things and try new activities? Is she constantly asking questions? Does she seem ready to interact more with others her own age? Preschool offers intellectual and physical stimulation that children may not get at home and opportunities to explore a new environment.

Socialization

In preschool, kids get to be around others their own age and learn how to behave in a group setting. This includes learning to share, waiting their turn, sitting calmly during story time, and raising their hand before speaking. When children are able to interact with a stable group of kids over time (as opposed to meeting new kids at the playground every day), they learn to be more socially adept and to communicate and work together. They learn that their actions have an effect on others and that the world is larger than just themselves. Preschool also gives them a chance to make friends their own age and feel a sense of identity with their classmates.

Independence

In a preschool environment, your child will become more independent and develop important self-help skills. You'll be amazed to see her take off her own coat and hang it on her hook or put materials away when she's done with an activity. By having some time away from their parents, kids practice being individuals in the world and relying on themselves. They make choices about what to play and whom to play with. They also get a chance to trust and bond with other adults and learn that they can survive without their parents. Preschool helps kids become more self-sufficient and more confident about making their own decisions.

Learning

Preschool offers an age-appropriate curriculum that helps kids prepare for kindergarten. In other words, children learn by being taught concepts and doing activities suitable to their age and level of development. The teachers help prepare children to learn to read and write by reading to them; playing rhyming games; and providing lots of books, paper, and drawing materials. Activities such as pouring cups of water into different sized containers over a water activity table form the foundation for understanding basic math concepts. Studies show that children who went to preschool enter kindergarten with better pre-reading and pre-math skills. When kids play with a wide variety of tools (e.g., play dough and puzzles) and outdoors on playground equipment, they're also learning coordination and developing their motor skills.

The most important benefit children can gain from preschool is a love for learning and for school. Preschool gives them a chance to understand how school works and what routines to expect, to make friends and get along with others, and to explore the world in a safe, fun, and age-appropriate way.

Benefits to Parents

Preschool can have benefits for parents as well. For working parents or a stay-at-home mom or dad who needs a few hours a week to her- or himself, preschool is a reliable source of child care. It can also be a good way to meet other families. As your child makes new friends, you'll meet their parents. You chose your preschool carefully and for reasons that work for your child and your family, and so did the parents of the other kids in the class. Preschool can be a way to meet people with whom you can share the experience of raising children the same age.

IS PRIVATE PRESCHOOL MY ONLY OPTION? IS THERE PUBLIC PRESCHOOL?

Almost all states have free, state-funded public preschool programs, though most are targeted at children who come from low-income families or who have disabilities or developmental delays. Spaces in these schools for children who don't meet preferred criteria may be very limited or unavailable, and families of children who don't meet the criteria are usually charged tuition. Only a small handful of states offer universal preschool to all children in the state at no cost, though these tend to be part-time programs for four-year-olds.

There are, however, public school districts throughout the country that offer preschool to the general population. The types of program vary from district to district. Some are free; others are tuition based. Some are half-day programs, and others offer a full-day schedule with extended care available. The minimum age to enroll may be from two and a half years to four years. Some schools give preference to children who live in the immediate neighborhood, come from low-income families, or have special needs. At programs with high demand, children may be admitted on a first-come, first-serve basis or through a lottery system.

To find out whether a public preschool is available where you live, whether your child is eligible, and how to apply, contact your local school district. You can also find out whether public pre-K is available in your state and check out the eligibility requirements at the Education Commission of the States' website (www.ecs.org/dbsearches/ Map_Searches/SRCH_ DB_EarlyLearning.htm) or in the National Institute for Early Education Research's *State Preschool Yearbook*, which is published each year and can be found at www.nieer.org.

For most people who want to send their child to preschool, it will have to be a privately run program. What does that

Real Parents Talk

When my son turned four and was old enough for the pre-K program at the public school, we decided to send him there two days a week in addition to his three days at the private school he had been enrolled at since he was two. We hope this will help us make an informed decision when it comes time to choosing which school to continue attending for kindergarten. Obviously, the cost difference between the two programs is significant, but we're finding that the fundamentals of what he's learning are essentially the same (like self-help skills and how to be a good friend). Both are building an excellent foundation for him for kindergarten.

—Liz H., Dedham, Massachusetts

mean? A private school is defined as a school that isn't administered by the government or funded by tax dollars. It selects its own student body and charges tuition to cover all or part of the costs. The terms *private* and *independent* are often used interchangeably, though there is a slight difference. Although a private school may be affiliated with and funded by another organization, such as a church or for-profit corporation, a truly independent board of trustees detached from any other organization governs an independent school.

WHAT IS HEAD START?

Head Start is a free, federally funded pre-K program available nationwide that helps prepare at-risk, low-income children for success in elementary school. The purpose of the program is to improve the lives of low-income children by providing a high-quality education as well as healthcare services, with a focus on parent education and involvement. If you think you may qualify, contact your local Head Start program for the eligibility requirements and to learn what's available to you. You can search for the nearest program at the website for the Administration for Children and Families of the U.S. Department of Health and Human Services (http://eclkc.ohs.acf.hhs.gov/hslc).

How Do I Know If My Child Is Ready for Preschool?

Although many preschools will start accepting children at the ages of two or two and a half, that doesn't mean that your child is suddenly ready for preschool when she reaches that age. Preschool readiness is more about where your child is developmentally. Is she ready from a social, emotional, cognitive, and physical standpoint to take part in a classroom environment with a group of other kids? Your child is most likely ready for her first early education experience if she shows the following signs of preschool readiness:

- She's okay spending time away from you or her other primary caregivers.
- She can play by herself for short periods of time, can follow simple instructions, and can focus on one task (such as coloring or doing a puzzle) for several minutes.
- She can participate in group activities with other kids, like sitting in circle time singing songs or listening to a story, and play cooperatively with others. Most preschool-age kids don't want to share and take turns all the time, but she should understand the concept and that it's appropriate behavior.
- She can express her wants and needs through words (not just crying), and ask questions.
- She's fairly independent or starting to be. Can she take care of some basic needs, like washing her hands and eating by herself?
- Many preschools require that kids be potty trained, although the occasional accident is expected.

These are just general guidelines. Every school has its own expectations and understands that three- and four-year-olds have different abilities from two-year-olds. So it's OK if your child doesn't do all these things yet. If you're thinking, "What

Real Parents Talk

I knew he was ready for preschool when he began climbing the walls at home—literally. He would try to climb our bookshelves to find new toys or games to play. We figured it was time for some new stimulation.

—Gail S., Pittsburgh, Pennsylvania

my child does best is play with dolls and eat sand," don't worry. Remember, she doesn't have to be ready for preschool when you're applying, but you can help her develop the skills she'll need for a successful school experience before she starts. You'll learn more about this in chapter 13, "Preschool Readiness Skills."

So How Do I Get Started?

When you start looking at preschools, there's much to think about. What's important to you in a program? What kind of approach will work best for your child? When should you start applying? In the next chapter, we'll talk about the time line for researching and applying and about how to stay organized throughout the process.

CHAPTER 2

Getting Organized

To give yourself enough time to research and visit all the preschool programs that interest you, you'll need to start the hunt for preschools early (we'll define *early* in just a bit). Being organized and planning ahead are essential for staying on top of deadlines for the different programs you're considering, as each one will have its own admissions process and time lines.

This chapter will help you take control of the process, give you a general time line to follow, and offer tips for putting all the pieces in order. You'll be less stressed and better able to reach your goal—finding the best nursery school for your child.

IT'S NEVER TOO EARLY

You're probably wondering, "How early do I need to start?" It's a good idea to begin researching preschool programs at least a year before you plan to enroll your child. So if a school has a September start date, start looking during the summer of the previous year. The more time you have to ask friends for recommendations, do research online, and go on school tours, the better prepared you'll be to make a decision about where to send your child. And if you're applying to selective schools that can't admit everyone, the more prepared you are, the more likely you are to get your child into the school you have your heart set on.

Although a year in advance may sound like plenty of time, if there are schools in your area with long waiting lists, you may want to start your preschool search much earlier. Almost every preschool with a waiting list starts accepting applications the day a child is born. As ridiculous as it sounds, a few nursery schools and all day cares will let you sign up while you're pregnant. This is not to say you should be filling out application forms in your postpartum room, but in general, the sooner you place your child on a waiting list, the better off you are. A spot at a high-quality program can be a hot commodity, and you want to make sure you give yourself enough time to research schools and decide where to apply so you can get your child on the lists of the schools you prefer. It's all about maximizing your options.

> **Real Parents Talk**
>
> Since we were interested in programs that started at two years old, we started looking for preschools when our son was only six months old and had to send in our applications when he was only one!
>
> —Bea W., Brookline, Massachusetts

Many nursery schools, however, and possibly every school in your neighborhood, don't start enrolling kids until just a few months before the first day of school in September. Some schools have the capacity to take new students throughout the year. And even if you're a little late to the process (perhaps you just moved to the area or recently decided to enroll your child in preschool), there are still things you can do to secure a spot (see chapter 11, "Our Child Didn't Get a Spot at Any Preschool—What Are Our Options?").

PRESCHOOL SEARCH TIME LINE

One of the challenging things about looking for a preschool is keeping on top of enrollment procedures for all the different programs you're considering, as each school has its own processes, requirements, and deadlines. The following time line will help you get a big-picture view of the whole preschool search process. The chapters that follow will go into each step in more detail. This is just to get you started—be sure to adjust it to your own particular needs.

As Early as Possible (If Applying to Preschools with Waiting Lists)

If preschools in your area have waiting lists, you'll want to start your search as early as possible. The sooner you put your child on a school's waiting list, the better are your chances of getting a spot.

- **Determine your preschool selection criteria.** Think about what you want in a preschool for your child: location, schedule, educational philosophy, cost, and so on.
- **Research potential preschools.** Find programs that fit your criteria by asking other parents, searching the Internet, checking out a local preschool guide, attending a preschool fair, and browsing school websites.
- **Visit schools.** For schools with waiting lists, call and ask to make an appointment for a visit.

- **Request waiting-list application forms.** Fill them out, and return them as soon as possible to be sure your child has an early spot on the list.
- **Follow up.** Call the schools again about a week after submitting the application forms to be sure they were received.

The Year before Your Child Will Enroll

Although it's not too late to apply to waiting-list schools, one year before your child will enroll is also the time to focus on all preschools. Application forms are usually due the December, January, or February prior to the school's September start date.

Spring and Summer

- **Determine your preschool selection criteria.** Consider the characteristics you'd like a program to have, such as a specific location, class size, price range, schedule, or educational philosophy.
- **Research potential preschools.** Locate preschools that meet your needs by talking to friends, checking out a local preschool guide, browsing online preschool directories, and visiting school websites.
- **Attend a preschool fair.** Many communities offer preschool fairs at which you can pick up brochures from several schools all at once and chat with preschool directors, teachers, and admissions representatives.

Fall and Winter

- **Contact schools.** Call the schools you're interested in and find out whether they have tours or open houses. If not, schedule an appointment to visit individually. When you call, be sure to ask about the admissions process and the school's birthday cutoff.
- **Visit schools.** Visit every school you're interested in. Be prepared with questions to ask that will help you determine whether the program is a good match for your child.
- **Pick up application forms.** Request forms from all the preschools you're considering. Some will let you download them from their website.
- **Submit application forms.** Turn in all the required paperwork before the deadline. If your top-choice school lets your child enroll at this point without going through a formal admissions process, congratulations—you're all set for preschool!
- **Financial aid.** If you're going to apply for financial aid, be sure to do so early in the process. Many schools have a session on financial aid information to help guide you through the process. Be sure to complete your forms and turn them in well before the deadline.
- **Child and parent interviews.** If the school requires a child or a parent interview, schedule one promptly.
- **Submit evaluation forms and recommendation letters.** If your child already attends preschool, you may need to submit an evaluation form from a current teacher. Although a personal letter of recommendation is not required, you can ask a person associated with the school to write one on your child's behalf.

- **Follow up.** If your child is on the waiting list at a school, call the school to inquire about his status and when they think a spot might open up.

The Year Your Child Will Enroll

Most preschools notify parents of their admissions status in the spring before the September your child starts school. Those with waiting lists may call a few days to a few months in advance to let you know your child has secured a spot.

Spring and Summer

- **Notification arrives.** Schools mail their notification letters to let you know whether your child has been accepted, rejected, or put on the waiting list.
- **The waiting list.** If your child is placed on the waiting list at your top-choice school, call to let the school know you're still interested. Of the schools your child was admitted to, choose your favorite and accept the spot.
- **Follow-up visit.** If your child is offered a space in a school but you're not sure if you want to send him there, call right away to see whether you can schedule a second visit.
- **Accept the offer.** When you've made your decision, send in the contract and tuition deposit by the deadline.
- **Notify the other schools.** If other schools accepted or wait-listed your child, be sure to let them know that he is going to another school so they can give that space to someone else on the waiting list. It's common courtesy as well as good karma!

TIPS FOR KEEPING ORGANIZED

Because there's no standard admissions time line, it's important to be organized if you're applying to more than a few nursery schools. Staying organized and keeping track of deadlines throughout the preschool search will help keep you from being stressed out.

- **Mark your calendar with all your important deadlines.** When you learn dates for preschool fairs, school tours, application and financial aid deadlines, and so on, jot them down.
- **Create a filing system to keep track of each school's paperwork.** Set up a folder (or just use paper clips) for each preschool you're applying to. This will help you keep all the brochures, your notes from school visits, copies of applications, and any other paperwork all in one place.
- **Make checklists.** To keep track of each school's deadlines and all the things you need to do, create a checklist.

Here's an example:

Little Sprouts Preschool

Action	Date	Completed
Call school to request application and arrange tour	September 2	✓
Go on school tour	October 14	✓
Write thank-you note	Before October 17	✓
Ask day care to fill out recommendation form	Before end of November	
Application due	December 14	
Recommendation form from day care due	December 14	

Action	Date	Completed
Schedule child and parent interviews	School will call	
Child interview and parent interview	January 24 or 25	
Admission letter mailed	Mid-March	

You can always make adjustments to this system to suit your own situation. The important thing is to have a system that works for you and to use it!

CHAPTER 3

Choosing a Preschool: The Basics

WHEN YOU FIRST START THINKING about what to look for in a preschool, you might be thinking, "Finger painting, building blocks, snack time. How complicated can it be?"

But just like choosing a college or deciding which company to work for, there are actually some big differences to consider among programs. There are part-time and full-time programs, and some that let you choose either one. Some schools emphasize social and emotional skills, and others focus more on the ABCs and 123s. Some require kids to be potty trained to attend, but others don't.

This chapter will cover the basic criteria to consider when beginning your preschool search, and chapter 5 will look at more program-specific differences that will help you evaluate various programs. Starting your preschool search by looking at the basics—practical considerations such as location, cost, minimum age to enroll, your child's personality, and your educational goals for her—will help you identify the programs that best suit your family. Take the schedule, for example. If you need full-time child care, then part-time nursery schools without after-school care are out! By recognizing your basic criteria early on, you can eliminate a bunch of programs from consideration and focus on the ones that fit your needs.

KNOW YOUR CHILD AND YOUR FAMILY

The most important factor in selecting a preschool is fit. Choosing a preschool is about finding the best fit for your child, your family, and the school—one that matches your child's personality and temperament, as well as your own needs and parenting values.

Consider Your Child's Personality and Needs

The key to finding the right preschool is understanding your child's personality and temperament. Each child is a unique individual with her own interests, capabilities, and needs, and these characteristics will help you determine the type of environment in which she'll learn best. Observing how your child responds to different settings—at the playground, in toddler classes, and at home—will help you figure out what you want to look for in a future preschool.

Think about your child's needs:

- Is she fairly self-sufficient or does she need a lot of one-on-one attention?
- Does she need a lot of structure, or does she prefer having many choices of activities?
- How does she respond to being in small and large groups?
- Does she get upset when left with a caregiver she doesn't know well?

- Is she very social? Does she like to interact with other kids, or does she prefer to play on her own?
- How well does she follow directions?
- Is she very active, and does she need a lot of time outdoors?
- Does she have a special interest in a particular activity, like music, art, or make-believe play?

Also, consider whether you want a school that matches your child's personality or one that challenges her to adjust to something different. If your child has trouble separating from you, you might consider a program that's only a few hours a week and that has a slow, gradual transition period in the beginning of the school year. However, you may choose to enroll her in a full-time program so she gets to know her teachers well and learns to trust other adults. If you have a shy child, will she be uncomfortable in a large, boisterous class or will it challenge her to develop her social skills?

If possible, you should look for a program that suits your child's temperament while encouraging her to develop other skills. If your child likes to move from activity to activity, for example, a program with lots of free play and some structured activities throughout the day will give her not only the opportunity to explore the classroom but also the chance to learn to sit still and participate in structured group activities.

Naturally, if your child is very young and won't start preschool for a few years, you can focus more on finding the preschool that fits your own needs and goals as a parent.

Consider Your Family's Needs and Values

In addition to your child's personality, you'll want to think about your own needs as parents and the characteristics of your family. For example, if you're a single parent or if both parents work full-time, a program with after-school care that provides lunch might be the most convenient option. Choosing a school close to your home above all other factors may be the best option if your family has close ties to the neighborhood community. If you're looking forward to meeting other families and forming friendships, you might want to look at schools with an active parent community and many organized social events.

Also, consider your parenting goals and values. Are you looking for a situation that emphasizes social and emotional development (like sharing, taking turns, and developing relationships with peers)? Or are you looking for one that has more of an academic focus (emphasizing math and reading concepts)? Do you want your child to be exposed to racial, socioeconomic, or other types of diversity at school? Is it important to you that your child learn to speak another language or learn about your religion?

> ### Real Parents Talk
>
> Having a Jewish curriculum was the most important element to us and therefore the only places we considered. Both of our boys now attend the preschool affiliated with our synagogue.
>
> —Cary K., San Mateo, California

No matter what your preferences and goals are, it's best to prioritize what you're looking for in a preschool program before you begin sorting through all the options.

AT WHAT AGE DO I WANT MY CHILD TO START PRESCHOOL?

Because preschool isn't mandatory, you have some flexibility here. Some preschools enroll kids as young as two years old, but most want children who are at least two and a half or three on or by a particular cutoff date. Most children start preschool when they're three or four, attend for one or two years, and then begin kindergarten at the age of five. Depending on your child's birthday and the cutoff dates at her preschool and the kindergarten she'll be attending, she may go to preschool for an additional year.

As an example, suppose your child's birthday is October 1:

- The minimum age to enroll at her preschool is two years and nine months by September 1.
- When she begins preschool in September, she'll be two years and eleven months old.
- The two elementary schools you're considering have different kindergarten cutoff dates: the private school requires kindergartners to be five years old by September 1, but the public school doesn't require children to turn five until December 1.

In this situation, your child could go to preschool for two or three years depending on which kindergarten she attends. The chart on the following page illustrates both scenarios.

Age Cutoff Example

	Age on September 1	Age on December 1	Preschool or Kindergarten
Year 1	2 years, 11 months	3 years, 2 months	First year of preschool
Year 2	3 years, 11 months	4 years, 2 months	Second year of preschool
Year 3	4 years, 11 months	5 years, 2 months	After two years of preschool, your child can enroll in the kindergarten that requires children to be five years old by December 1
Year 4	5 years, 11 months	6 years, 2 months	After three years of preschool, your child can enroll in the kindergarten that requires children to be five years old by September 1

When deciding at what age to enroll your child into pre-school, you may also want to consider how many years you'd like her to attend before going on to kindergarten. For instance, even though the school of your choice takes two-year-olds, you may opt to enroll your child when she's three so that she attends only for two years rather than three. Maybe you want to keep your child at home with you or a caregiver for another year, you're happy with her small family day care, or you'd rather wait to start paying school tuition. There's no right or wrong answer. When deciding when your child should start, however, take into account that if you do decide to wait to apply a year or two after the cutoff age, there will probably be fewer slots open, as kids who have already enrolled will have taken most of them.

As we talked about in chapter 1, bear in mind that simply because your child is old enough to start nursery school, that

When our kids were three, we sent them to a small, play-based program to give them a fun introduction to school and get them used to spending some time away from Mommy. Once they turned four, we chose a more traditional pre-K program with a bit more structure. Now they're learning their letters, practicing writing their name, learning cutting skills, and so on, while still doing fun activities like crafts and nature walks.

—Elaine H., Woodbridge,
New Jersey

doesn't mean that she's necessarily ready to go. If you're not sure, take another look at the questions in that section to help you decide.

With so many types of programs to choose from, keep in mind that it's possible for your child to experience more than one. If you believe that your two-year-old needs more stimulation but isn't ready for a large, structured program, she could start by taking several drop-off classes or going to a small, part-time preschool and then transitioning to a bigger, full-time program if you determine that would be a better fit the following year.

SHOULD WE DELAY KINDERGARTEN?

Generally speaking, most children are ready for kindergarten at the age of five. However, some kids need an extra year to mature or reach certain developmental milestones. During the last year of preschool, your child's teachers will be able to tell you if they think your child needs an extra year of preschool before starting kindergarten.

Some nursery schools allow children to stay until the age of five and a half or six. A few preschools, as well as some elementary schools, offer a separate transitional kindergarten class for this age group that acts as a bridge between preschool and kindergarten (see chapter 1). If your preschool doesn't accommodate older kids, however, you'll need to find another program that does.

Some parents think it will give their child an advantage to wait another year before starting kindergarten, particularly if he or she is one of the youngest in the class. (After all, wouldn't it be better to be older, bigger, and smarter than everyone else?) This practice is known as "redshirting." The latest research shows that redshirting doesn't give children any practical advantage or improve their school success in the long term. In fact, how well children are able to learn and absorb information from their teacher is not driven by age, but rather by how well-prepared they are by preschool and their home environment. Kids who have been redshirted can also feel out of place with younger kids and bored by schoolwork that's too easy for them.

If you think your child doesn't seem quite ready for kindergarten, talk to your preschool teacher—you may have good reason to wait a year. If your child is developmentally on track and you're just looking for a competitive advantage, however, redshirting may not be the answer.

WHAT'S THE BEST LOCATION?

Do you want the school to be close to your home? Close to your office? Near Grandma's house? How far are you willing to drive to drop off and pick up your child?

The nice thing about a school in your own neighborhood (besides the short commute) is that chances are lots of the other kids live nearby, too. That makes it easier to arrange playdates or run into the other kids at the local playground. There's also a good chance that the same kids will end up in elementary school together, which gives your child ready-made friends when kindergar-

ten rolls around. The advantages of choosing a preschool close to your office are that you can spend your commute time with your child and can get to school quickly for an event (or an emergency).

If you'll be driving your child to school, check how easy it is to park or see if there are dedicated five-minute pickup and drop-off parking spots. Some schools have curbside drop-off in which teachers transport kids directly from the car to the classroom and vice versa (and you thought only fast-food outlets had drive-through service).

You might think it's reasonable to drive forty-five minutes each way to send your child to a preschool you love—until you actually have to do it every day. It might not be worth all the back and forth and extra gasoline, especially if your child's on a half-day schedule. Some parents in this situation opt not to bother driving back home and instead use the time to go to the gym or run errands near the school. Consider doing a test drive during the week to see how long the ride will really take. Driving to the school on a Sunday afternoon won't give you a realistic idea of what traffic is going to be like during rush hour!

WHAT SCHEDULE WORKS BEST FOR OUR FAMILY?

Preschool schedules range from half days a few days a week to full days, five days a week. Part-time programs are less expensive and may let you choose from a few schedules (like Monday, Wednesday, and Friday mornings, for instance). Be sure that the hours will work for your schedule. Be aware that some schools will charge a late-pickup fee of as much as a dollar per minute.

Part Time

Half-day (approximately two to four hours) or short-week programs are good for some children. They get more downtime, maybe a longer nap, and are available for other activities or playdates when they're not at school. A part-time setting also makes for a gradual transition to kindergarten for kids (or parents) who may not be ready for full-time school. Adding more hours as your child becomes more comfortable or gets closer to kindergarten is always an option as well. Think about your child's natural schedule. When does she nap? Is she cranky in the mornings? Keep in mind, children are very adaptable and can easily adjust to a new schedule in a matter of weeks. And because most parents prefer mornings, if you're open to afternoons, you may find more spaces available.

Full Time

A full-time program (five or more hours a day, five days a week) gives preschoolers the opportunity to explore and play in the classroom every day. It can seem like a lot of time for a young child, but many children thrive on the continuity. Kids make friends easily and come to feel a strong sense of community because they see one another every day. If you have a scheduling conflict or don't want your child in school as long as the program hours, you can ask whether there's any flexibility in the schedule. Some full-time programs give you the option of picking your child up at an earlier time each day or sending your child less than five days a week (this doesn't necessarily mean a break in tuition, however, so be sure to ask).

Occasionally, there are special circumstances in which parents end up sending their child to two different preschools on alternate days (Monday, Wednesday, and Friday at one school and Tuesday and Thursday at another, for example). This could be because they couldn't get a full-time slot at their first-choice school or because one school offers something the other doesn't, like a language-immersion program.

Extended Care

Many programs offer extended care before and after school to accommodate working parents. So even if the official school day ends at 2:30 p.m., for instance, after-school care may be available until 6:00 p.m. for an extra fee. Before enrolling your child in extended care, be sure to understand the hours, cost, and types of activities that take place. Find out if it's necessary to sign up in advance. Some programs offer after-school enrichment classes (typically for an additional fee) like gymnastics, music, or cooking.

Academic Year versus Year-Round

Some preschools follow an academic year (around September to June) and either close over the summer or offer an optional summer camp. If your preschool closes for the summer but you still need child care during those months, you could always enroll your child in a summer camp at another school or a recreation center.

Other schools run throughout the calendar year, with a short one- or two-week vacation during the summer. If you're looking at a year-round program but want your child to do something different during the summer, make sure this won't mean losing your spot. Some schools will accept a holding fee to keep your child's place over the summer.

> ### Real Parents Talk
>
> The main thing for us was flexibility in the program schedule. We found a place where we could choose to send our daughter a few days one week and all five days the next week or substitute days (a Tuesday for Thursday, for example) to fit our work schedules.
>
> —Sucharita M., Charlotte, North Carolina

Holiday and Vacation Schedules

Every preschool closes for major holidays and takes winter and spring (and sometimes fall) breaks. They also have certain days throughout the year when they're closed for teacher professional development days, parent-teacher conferences, or other special events. On those days, some nursery schools offer optional day camps for the kids in lieu of a regular school day. If both parents work, you'll need to plan ahead for child care on the days when the preschool is closed and doesn't offer a day camp.

HOW MUCH CAN WE AFFORD TO PAY FOR PRESCHOOL?

It would be great to be able to say, "For my child, money is no object!" but that's not realistic for many families. Before deciding on a preschool, examine your family finances and know what you can afford. Nursery school tuition varies widely and can range anywhere from a few hundred dollars a month to upward of $20,000 for the school year in large metropolitan areas. Schools may increase the tuition whenever they choose, and some do it every year.

Tuition covers most of the costs of running the school, from teacher salaries and benefits to operating expenses like heat and electricity. Just as cost-of-living expenses vary from one city to another, so does preschool tuition. In addition to location, the amount will depend on the preschool's schedule and offerings. You'll naturally pay more for a program that's full time versus part time, has a lower teacher-student ratio, or a foreign-language specialist who comes in twice a week. Co-op programs in which parents commit volunteer hours to help run the school (see chapter 5) won't set you back as much as a school that doesn't require any parent participation. Schools also differ in terms of what costs are included in the tuition, such as lunch, snacks, and field trips.

But that's just tuition. Add in the registration and materials fees, before- and after-school care, enrichment classes, and day camps, and your actual expenses can quickly add up. Private schools may also charge families additional fees to help pay for building upgrades or to buy out of the volunteer commitment. Many programs also actively solicit donations, so find out whether you're expected to contribute. If the school's brochure or website mentions the importance of fundraising to cover operating expenses or that parents are asked to make an annual gift, you should expect to make a donation in addition to tuition payments.

Although cost is a major factor, you shouldn't automatically rule out any school just because of high tuition. Financial aid may well be available. To be on the safe side, however, be sure to apply to some schools you know you can afford as well as the schools with higher tuition. You'll learn more about figuring out your preschool budget, financial aid, and other strategies to help pay for preschool in chapter 12.

Withdrawal Policy

If there's a chance you might withdraw your child from preschool or change schools before or during the school year, be sure to find out your school's withdrawal policy. Many schools require a nonrefundable tuition deposit, so don't be surprised if you don't get your deposit money back if you change your mind and decide not to send your child there (say, if she gets off the waiting list somewhere else or you decide to move).

At year-round schools, which parents typically pay for on a monthly basis, parents are often required to provide written notification a month or so prior to the withdrawal date and may be charged a one- or two-month tuition penalty fee

> ### Real Parents Talk
>
> There are definitely some highly prestigious, expensive preschools out there but we decided not to look at anything too costly. It is, after all, only preschool and we don't feel we need to spend college tuition rates to have him start his education off on the right foot.
>
> —Karen L., San Francisco, California

on top of that. At some preschools that follow an academic year, the entire year's tuition becomes nonrefundable after a set date (e.g., July 1), so if you withdraw your child anytime during the school year (or even before the first day), you may still be obligated to pay for the balance of the year. These schools may make exceptions for special situations such as moving out of the area, the child becoming seriously ill, or if they find a new student to fill the child's spot. Every school has its own withdrawal policy, so be sure you understand the details before signing the contract.

Tuition-refund insurance may also be available for a fee— this plan provides families with partial- or full-refund payments in the event you leave the school. The insurance typically does not cover all withdrawals, however, and often will not provide coverage until your child has attended the school for some period (e.g., fourteen school days), so be sure to read the terms carefully.

By understanding your fundamental preferences for choosing a nursery school, the selection process will go more smoothly, and you'll save yourself a lot of time, effort, and fees. The more you know what you're looking for, the easier it will be to find the school that's best for your child. The next chapter will discuss additional criteria you'll want to focus on when researching schools.

CHAPTER 4

What to Look for in a Preschool

ALTHOUGH PRACTICAL CONSIDERATIONS WILL GUIDE your preschool search, there are many other factors to think about when choosing ultimately where to enroll your child. This chapter will help you understand some of the characteristics of preschool programs and why they might factor into your decision-making process. But keep in mind that there are a million things you could consider—only you can decide which are the most important. The following selection criteria are here to help spur your thinking about what you'd most like to see in a program and to help you narrow down all the nursery school choices to a handful.

WHAT IS THE CLASSROOM LIKE?

Mixed-Age versus Same-Age Classes

In some schools, kids of different ages are all in one class together. Mixed-age classrooms give younger kids an opportunity to learn from the older ones. Older children benefit from the opportunity to become leaders, which builds their self-esteem and teaches them to help and nurture the younger kids. Because children stay with the same teacher for several years, they get to develop a close relationship, and the teacher gets a chance to know the children's learning style very well.

Other schools split children into same-age groups (such as twos, threes, and fours). The kids are generally at the same place developmentally, and teachers can plan programs and activities specific to that age group.

In either scenario, what matters most is that teachers strive to understand where each child is developmentally, regardless of age, so that they can tailor activities to support and extend their learning.

Class Size

Smaller classes for preschoolers mean more individual attention and a less chaotic classroom. If your child is uncomfortable in a big crowd or in noisy settings, you may want to look for a preschool with small classes. However, if your child likes to be around lots of kids, he might do well in a larger class. Where there are more kids, there are more friends to play with! Of course, a lot depends on the individual teacher and the teacher-student ratio in the class. Your child is certainly better off in a class with twenty-four kids and three very experienced,

> ### Real Parents Talk
>
> The large size of our son's class is not an issue as the teacher has very good control of the classroom. Having more children turned out to be a bonus since it allowed him to make more compatible friends. With smaller classes, there might've been less of a chance of this happening.
>
> —Shally S., Los Angeles, California

nurturing teachers than in a small class with seven kids and a teacher who isn't as qualified or motivated. The National Association for the Education of Young Children (NAEYC) recommends a class size of eighteen or less for two-and-a-half- or three-year-olds and twenty or less for four-year-olds.

Teacher-Student Ratio

The teacher-student ratio refers to the number of students per teacher. If you have a class with two teachers and twenty students, the teacher-student ratio is 1:10. A low teacher-student ratio means more one-on-one attention for your child. Not all the adults in a classroom have to be full teachers, as some can be teacher assistants or student teachers. The NAEYC recommends a 1:9 or lower ratio for two-and-a-half- or three-year-olds and a 1:10 or lower ratio for four-year-olds.

Special Programs

Schools may offer special programs beyond the regular classroom experience. Although all teachers incorporate some music and art in the curriculum, some schools offer these and other classes, such as physical education or foreign language, that are taught by specialists who come in once or twice a week. A school that puts an emphasis on nature may have kids spend much of the day outdoors, or a school located in a community center may offer swimming lessons. Some take the kids on weekly or monthly field trips. A preschool attached to an elementary school may have a buddy program in which each child is paired with an older student who reads and does activities with him. Special programs are great, and if you find a school that offers them, that's terrific. But try to think of these programs as extra, and don't let them overshadow other important criteria, such as the quality of the teachers.

Preschool Size

Some preschools have just a handful of kids in a single class. Others have more than a hundred students divided into several classrooms. The size of the school will have less impact on your child than the teacher-student ratio in the child's own classroom, but it will have an effect on your experience as a parent. Whether it's a large or a small class, you'll probably get to know the teachers and the parents of every child in your kid's classroom pretty well. At a larger school, you and your child might get a chance to also meet families outside of the class, so there is potential for meeting others you can connect with. You'll just need to make a little effort to get to know them.

WHAT ARE THE TEACHERS LIKE?

One of the hardest things to learn when looking at preschools—and yet probably the most important—is the quality of the teachers and whether they're the kind of people you want teaching and caring for your child. Depending on the class size, a preschool room will generally have a head teacher and sometimes another teacher and teacher assistant. Use your judgment and your people instincts when you meet the teachers.

> ### Real Parents Talk
>
> After talking to friends whose kids were in preschool, we realized that a good teacher should be the number-one criteria. Your kid can be in the best school possible, but if he or she has a mediocre teacher, the school's reputation will not make up for this.
>
> —Miguel P., Newport News, Virginia

Do they really seem to enjoy being around children? Is the head teacher someone you can talk to about your concerns? Do the kids in the class seem to have a strong attachment to the teachers? Find out as much as you can about the teachers and what the parents think of them, as they will play a vital role in your child's development and in making your child's experience a good one.

Educational Background

Although the formal training required of preschool teachers varies widely from state to state, teachers should have a minimum of a two-year associate's degree. Some formal training in early childhood education, which provides training in child development, observing and assessing kids, and teaching a preschool curriculum, is also a good sign. Many nursery schools require teachers to hold a bachelor's or master's degree and be certified in early childhood education. If the assistants don't have the same qualifications, that's fine, as long as they have some specialized training and are good with children.

It's a good sign if teachers have an impressive educational background and many years of experience behind them, but keep an open mind. You may come across educators who don't have a master's degree or years of teaching experience under their belt but are wonderful, caring, and effective preschool teachers who would be great for your child.

Teacher Turnover

How long have the teachers been with the program? How much turnover is there? Of course, even the best teachers may leave the best school for any number of personal reasons. But if more than a few leave every year, it may be that the teachers don't feel they're being treated well by the administration. And if the teachers aren't happy, it may not be the best environment for your child. Children do better with stability and need to be able to form strong relationships with their caregivers, so think twice about preschools where the teachers come and go frequently.

Personal Traits

Teachers are like second parents when your child is away from his family, so they should show a natural love for children, a desire to help them learn and grow, and plenty of patience. A good teacher will be warm, attentive, organized, and enthusiastic. Whether in the classroom or on the playground, they should always be engaged and helping kids to learn and explore, not just standing around watching. A good teacher also recognizes that different children have different needs. Such teachers should be able to adapt the curriculum for kids who are a little ahead as well as those who are a little behind.

Think about the traits that will be most important to your individual child, too. For instance, does he need lots of hugs, or does he prefer to have more personal space? If there's more than one classroom at the preschool, you might not have a say in which teacher your child has, so make sure you like them all!

HOW IS THE SCHOOL RUN?

Preschool Director

The preschool director is the person in charge of running the entire school. It's up to the director to recruit and hire the best staff, to motivate them, and to make sure they have the resources they need. The director is responsible for planning the curriculum, managing the budget, recruiting new families, ensuring that the facilities are kept up, and much more. The director also represents the school to the parents, prospective families, and the wider community.

When you visit the school, be sure you meet the director. Does he inspire confidence in you? Do the teachers and parents speak highly of him? Is he able to articulately describe the school's educational philosophy and values? Does he have good relationships with the families? Does he greet the kids by name? You want to feel confident that the school is operating smoothly and that the director is someone who will work with you if any issues arise.

Parent-Teacher Communication

Good communication between teachers and parents is hugely important. Consider how much information you want, how often, and how you'd like to hear from the school. Teachers should keep you in the loop about your child's social, emotional, and academic development. A good preschool will tell you what your child is learning, whether he's progressing, and how you can help. If your child is having any problems at school or home, his teacher can be a great source of support.

Ask how the preschool communicates with parents. How often are parent-teacher conferences? Is there a newsletter? Is it weekly or monthly? Are teachers available by phone or email? Will the teacher have time to touch base with you for a couple of minutes every day at drop-off or pickup? Many programs will also send written progress reports (a nicer, gentler school report card) so you can identify your child's social, physical, and academic strengths and learn about any areas he may need help with.

Licensing and Accreditation

Licensing

All preschools have to meet state licensing requirements, although regulations vary from state to state. Having a license doesn't ensure a high-quality preschool, but it does show that the program has met the state's health and safety standards in areas like teacher and director qualifications; the staff-to-child ratio; and number of staff trained in CPR, playground safety, and nutrition. Many states exempt religious-based preschools from some or all requirements (though many meet the standards anyway). You can check to see whether a preschool's license is up to date by contacting your state or county social services department, or just ask the school to see its license.

To learn more about your state's licensing requirements, visit the page "Child Center Requirements" at the website for the National Resource Center for Health and Safety in Child Care and Early Education (http://nrckids.org/STATES/states.htm).

Accreditation

The National Association for the Education of Young Children (NAEYC) administers the largest and most widely recognized accreditation system for early childhood programs such as preschools and child care centers. If a program is NAEYC accredited, that means it chose to apply for accreditation and then went through the process of identifying areas that don't meet accreditation standards, making any necessary improvements, going through an on-site visit by assessors to validate that the program meets all the standards, and being reviewed and approved by an accreditation panel of experts. Programs with accreditation meet high standards of quality set by the NAEYC that go well beyond most states' licensing requirements for teacher-student ratio, teacher qualifications and training, developmental appropriateness of curriculum, physical environment, and health and safety. All accredited programs are licensed, but not all licensed programs are accredited. Once accreditation is granted, programs have to reapply every five years to maintain this status.

Because the process is so rigorous and time consuming, fewer than one in ten preschools has NAEYC accreditation. If a school has this accreditation, you can be pretty confident that it's a high-quality program. However, there are also many excellent preschools that have simply not chosen to go through the accreditation process. You can search the NAEYC database for accredited preschools in your area and check out their guidelines at www.naeyc.org or its website for parents, www.rightchoiceforkids.org.

NAEYC QUALITY CRITERIA FOR EARLY EDUCATION PROGRAMS

The National Association for the Education of Young Children (NAEYC) began its accreditation system in 1985 with the goal of providing a system to measure and improve the quality of early education programs. Today, over eight thousand programs are NAEYC accredited. In order to earn accreditation, an early education program must meet high standards in the following areas:

- Promote positive relationships for all children and adults to encourage each child's sense of individual worth.
- Implement a curriculum that fosters all areas of child development: cognitive, emotional, language, physical, and social.
- Use developmentally, culturally, and linguistically appropriate and effective teaching approaches.
- Provide ongoing assessments of each child's learning and development and communicate the child's progress to the family.
- Promote the nutrition and health of children and protect children and staff from illness and injury.
- Employ and support a teaching staff who have the educational qualifications, knowledge, and professional commitment necessary to promote children's learning and development and to support families' diverse interests and needs.
- Establish and maintain collaborative relationships with each child's family.
- Establish relationships with and use the resources of the community to support the achievement of program goals.
- Provide a safe and healthy physical environment.
- Implement strong personnel, fiscal, and program management policies so that all children, families, and staff have high-quality experiences.

National Association for the Education of Young Children. (2008). NAEYC Accreditation: The Right Choice For Kids [Brochure]. Washington, D.C.

WHAT IS THE COMMUNITY LIKE?

Other Parents

Your child isn't the only one who'll be doing more socializing when preschool starts. You'll be spending a lot of time with the other parents at drop-off and pickup, playdates, birthday parties, and school events. Preschool is a great opportunity to meet and connect with other people with kids your child's age. If you're looking forward to meeting new people, choose a preschool with an active parent community. A good sign is an active parent or parent-teacher association that plans programs like family picnics, holiday parties, and parent-only social events. Many schools also have an online discussion board (such as Yahoo! Groups) where parents and teachers can email the entire class with questions or announcements, post photos, and coordinate volunteers.

Diversity

Consider how important it is for your child to meet and interact with children and staff from a diverse range of backgrounds, including differences in race, ethnicity, socioeconomic status, abilities, religion, and family structures. Preschoolers will start asking questions about people who look different from themselves or have a different type of family. A diverse preschool gives kids—and their parents—the opportunity to get to know many kinds of people. When children feel that their race, culture, and family structure are respected, they have a greater sense of belonging and develop more confidence and a positive self-image.

A preschool will demonstrate its commitment to diversity

through the makeup of its staff and students, and in its choices of activities, books, wall displays, and holiday celebrations.

Ask whether the program has a specific commitment to diversity, such as a diversity coordinator or committee dedicated to overseeing diversity initiatives, and how diversity is integrated into the curriculum. Even in neighborhoods that aren't very multicultural, diversity can be incorporated into the classroom in fun and interesting ways.

DEDICATED PRESCHOOL OR ONGOING SCHOOL?

Most preschools serve only prekindergarten students, although some are attached to elementary schools—these are also known as ongoing schools. If you plan to send your child to a private school for kindergarten, you may want to ask the preschool-only programs you're considering which private schools the children go on to attend. That could be an indication of which private schools the nursery school has a good relationship with. Talk to the staff and current parents to find out how helpful a preschool is with the kindergarten admissions process. It's very helpful to have a director and teachers who will recommend schools they think will suit your child and write thoughtful recommendation letters on his behalf.

If your child's preschool is part of an elementary school

(public or private), you're in luck. In almost all cases, enrollment in the preschool means automatic acceptance into the elementary school. This means that your child will have an easy time transitioning to kindergarten, because he'll already know his classmates and be in a familiar setting. For private schools, it also means you don't have to go through the kindergarten admissions process! In fact, at some private schools, enrolling in the preschool may be your only chance to get into the elementary school, as some schools fill up their kindergarten spots with their preschoolers. But check with the director to make sure that this is the school's policy and to see whether there is a kindergarten-readiness test. Also, be sure to do your research on the entire school. Just because the preschool may be high quality and a good fit for your child now, that doesn't necessarily mean that the quality and fit in higher grades will be as great.

However, a word of caution on private ongoing schools if there's a chance you may decide to send him to a different school once preschool is over (either to send him to a different private school or to public school). If you apply for admission to kindergarten at other private schools, you may not find your school director to be as helpful as you'd like with the application process. Also, if you plan on sending a younger sibling to the preschool in a few years, find out the sibling policy in advance. Not only does sibling preference usually not apply once the family leaves the school, but many ongoing schools are not as inclined to admit the younger siblings knowing the family isn't committed to staying for the long term.

FEEDER PRESCHOOLS—A LEG UP IN KINDERGARTEN ADMISSIONS?

You may hear that the private elementary school you have your eye on has feeder preschools, whose kids are presumed to have better odds when applying for kindergarten admission. Although in the past this may have been true, nowadays, private elementary schools strive for diversity and prefer that their kindergartners come from many different preschools. So even though it may help that the schools have a close relationship, don't count on going to a certain preschool guaranteeing your child admission into an elementary school.

In fact, because a kindergarten can take only so many kids from each preschool (and a preschool director will place calls to admissions directors for only so many students from the program), your child might have an advantage coming from an under-the-radar preschool where he's the only child applying rather than being one of a dozen applying to kindergarten from the same preschool.

If a feeder preschool is a great match for your child and you think he'll be happy and do well there, then being a feeder may tip the scale against an equally good preschool that doesn't have close ties to the elementary school. However, if the nursery school is a poor fit, your child might not have a good experience or develop the skills he'll need to be accepted into the kindergarten. So by all means, consider feeder schools for your child, but above all, think about your child's personality and needs when making your decision.

WHAT DOES THE ADMISSIONS PROCESS TELL YOU?

Application Process

The preschool application process varies from school to school (we'll go into more depth about that in chapter 8). When you're looking at different programs, make sure that you find out all the pertinent details so you know what to expect. There are preschools that will enroll your child after you fill out a one-page form with your contact information; there are also programs that require parents to write an essay and bring their child in to be interviewed. The interview could mean playing in a classroom with other kids or testing the child's knowledge of colors and shapes. Some schools don't charge an application fee; others make you pay just to apply, with no guarantee of being accepted. Think about how each school's admissions process feels to you as a family and about how much effort, money, and time you're willing to put into each application.

Sibling Policy

If you have (or plan on having) younger children, you'll want to learn about the preschool's sibling policy. Almost all schools give siblings of current students higher priority over new families in the admissions process. Depending on the program, sibling preference might or might not apply if both the younger and older siblings will not be enrolled at the same time (if the older one leaves for kindergarten the following year, for instance).

Keep in mind that a sibling preference policy does not necessarily mean admission is guaranteed. Though rare, there are instances where a nursery school may not accept a younger sibling because of the number of other sibling applicants, the child's developmental readiness, special needs the school may not be able to accommodate, or other factors. Some programs also take into account how involved the family has been in the school community.

In addition to admissions, find out whether the preschool offers a sibling discount. That can mean anywhere from a 5 percent to a 20 percent break on the younger child's tuition.

Special Needs

If your child has a disability or developmental delay, you'll want to be sure to find a preschool that can help him learn in an appropriate way. Every state has agencies that can assess children to determine whether they require special educational services. To find yours, ask your pediatrician or go to www.nichcy.org/Pages/StateSpecificInfo.aspx and contact the organization in your state listed under "Programs for Children with Disabilities: Ages 3 through 5." If your child is eligible, the agency will refer you to a free public preschool program that can accommodate his needs. This might be the right choice for you, or you might feel that his needs would be better met at a private preschool.

There are a few private preschools that serve only kids with special needs, and others combine kids with special needs and kids without them. In either environment, the staff should be specially trained to provide for each child's individual needs. The school should have small classes and offer more one-on-one attention than a traditional preschool. The school should also provide parents with information and support to help them understand how to nurture and educate their child.

Some mainstream private preschools will enroll your child, especially if the disability is not severe. Many preschool teachers and administrators are well informed about learning disabilities. Talk with them about whether their program is a good fit for your child. A program may require that an adult shadows your child while he's at school. Most, however, will be up front about letting you know whether they don't have the resources to give your child the individual attention he'll require for a good, fully integrated preschool experience.

The type and severity of your child's disability, along with your own priorities, will affect your choice. If your primary goal is just for your child to socialize with children without disabilities, a regular preschool may be fine. But if he needs a lot of help learning functional skills, like drinking out of a cup or asking to play with a toy, you may prefer a special education preschool that's designed to meet his needs. For more information on preschool special education, visit the website of the National Center for Learning Disabilities (www.ncld.org), or the National Dissemination Center for Children with Disabilities (www.nichcy.org).

PRESCHOOL SELECTION TIPS FOR
SPECIAL NEEDS CHILDREN

It might require some legwork on your part to find the right preschool, but your child deserves to be in a great program that will accommodate his challenges and build on his strengths. When researching programs, find out whether the school's policies match your child's requirements for the following:

· **Academics**. What does the school expect from students? A high-pressure learning environment in which children are taught to memorize the alphabet or required to sit and focus on a single task for a long period of time may be too stressful for a child with special needs.

· **Experience**. Ask what experience the school has in dealing with special needs kids, what kind of training the staff has, and what they can do to accommodate your child.

· **Inclusiveness**. Does the school welcome special needs kids or just tolerate them? What effort will be made to integrate your child into the rest of the class?

· **One-on-one attention.** Does the school have a low teacher-student ratio so your child gets the attention he needs? Even better, can it provide an aide to work with him individually? If the answer is no, ask whether you can hire someone for that role.

· **Public school**. Consider taking advantage of free public preschool programs that are designed with your child's needs in mind. These are usually half-day programs, but you might be able to have your child bused to another preschool for the afternoon if you need full-day care.

Talk with your pediatrician as well as the director and teachers at any preschool you're considering to find the best choice for your child's individual needs.

WHAT ARE THE SCHOOL POLICIES?

Every preschool has policies on things like potty training, separation, and discipline. You'll want to look for a program that shares your philosophy on these issues.

Potty Training

Each school approaches the potty training issue in its own way. Some insist that children be able to go to the bathroom on their own before they can be admitted to the school. They won't hold a few accidents in the beginning of the school year against them, however. Others are more flexible and will support toilet training as part of a child's learning. Child care centers and programs with a toddler class already change diapers and may be more understanding of children who toilet train a little later than their peers.

Oftentimes, parents find that having a deadline to get their child potty trained turns out to be the best thing that could have happened. Many find that it's faster and easier than they expected when they're really focused on helping their child learn to use the toilet. But if your child is a late bloomer in this regard, be sure to know the policy at the schools you're interested in and apply only to schools that don't require it.

Separation

For many toddlers and parents, being apart from each other for the first time is the most significant experience of starting preschool. How a preschool handles transition during the first few weeks (this is known as the phase-in period) varies considerably among schools. In the first couple of weeks, children need time to adjust to their new school situation and to feel comfortable with their teachers.

To make the transition go more smoothly, some schools offer an orientation session a few days before school starts so you and your child can check out the classroom and meet the teacher. Some preschools have a shorter schedule during the first few days and gradually go longer until the kids are used to the full-day schedule.

Some schools let parents stay in the classroom (or linger outside) after class begins if their child is having a hard time letting go. Teachers may allow this to go on for a few days or a few months, depending on the school. Others have firm rules that parents must drop off their child and leave before class starts.

All preschoolers must eventually make a healthy separation from their parents before they can adjust to the daily routine. But if the thought of being asked to leave your crying child makes you want to cry, you may need a preschool with a more flexible separation policy. Bear in mind, most kids stop crying soon after you leave. Some children might take a few minutes longer than others, but they don't spend hours crying when they're at school. (Parents have trouble believing this, but it's true.)

Discipline

Preschools have their own specific rules for handling disagreements among students and for students who misbehave. There will always be a time that a child doesn't want to share or forgets to use words to resolve a situation and hits somebody. Ask the school how it deals with these situations. Does it use time-outs or redirect the children to other activities? Does it help kids work out their disagreements or leave them to solve things on their own? If a child is crying, does someone pick him up, or sit with him, or leave him to calm down on his own? If a child leaves circle time to do a puzzle elsewhere in the room, how does the teacher handle that? If your child gets hurt, how will the school tell you about it? If another child was involved, will the teacher tell you who?

It's very important for you to feel comfortable with the school's philosophy for discipline. Most preschool teachers have a lot of knowledge and experience with what works and what doesn't. This doesn't mean they have to discipline the same way you do at home, but you should feel that you can trust the teacher's judgment and make sure that your child isn't getting mixed messages about what's OK and what isn't.

Meals

Find out whether the school serves meals and snacks or if you need to pack your child's lunch. If meals aren't included, the school may offer a meal service you can pay for per day or for the whole week. If you want to see what types of meals are offered, how nutritious they are, and whether there are vegetarian or other options, ask to see the lunch and snack menus.

If your child has a food allergy or you're sensitive to what he eats, ask whether there are any food restrictions. Many preschools don't allow peanut butter or other nut products because of allergies (sunflower butter is an acceptable alternative), and some don't allow sugary treats. Also, find out whether the school will send home your child's leftovers so you can see how much and what he ate. You'll find a list of lunch and snack ideas for preschoolers in chapter 14.

Parent Involvement

Most preschools operate on a pretty thin margin and need help from parents with everything from providing snacks and driving for field trips to planning major fundraising events and remodeling facilities. Find out what kind of parent involvement is welcomed or expected. Co-op schools, for instance, require a certain number of volunteer hours per month (see chapter 5). Some schools, particularly day cares, don't request or require any participation. Most are somewhere in between. If your schedule doesn't allow you to volunteer a lot, don't apply to schools that require it (or find schools that will let you pay a volunteer opt-out fee).

Classroom Drop-In

A school with an open-door policy welcomes parents to drop in anytime, unannounced, to observe or even participate in classroom activities. Many preschools, however, find that disruptive and prefer that you visit at designated times or make plans with the teacher ahead of time. Bear in mind that other kids might feel envious if one child's parent is in the classroom all the time and theirs aren't, and this could cause problems. Ask the staff what the policy is and talk to current parents during your school visit to see if they're comfortable with it.

Illnesses

Every preschool has a sick policy that explains which symptoms mean your child has to stay home from school and whether teachers will give medicine with your permission. Although you may not want your child around sick kids, are you OK with being called to pick him up every time he has a stuffy nose? Most schools will allow a child with a runny nose but no fever to come to school. If your child stays home or is sent home sick, he'll usually need to be free of fever or other serious symptoms for at least twenty-four hours before he can return to school.

Nap

If you're concerned about your child's nap (or lack thereof), ask about the school's nap schedule and policy. Almost all full-day and some half-day programs build a thirty-minute or hour nap time into their daily schedule. The school usually provides a mat or cot for each child to sleep on, though some schools require that children bring in their own mat. Some schools encourage bringing a huggable toy to school for nap time; others forbid it. If your child no longer naps, see whether he'll be allowed to play quietly or look at books instead. Some schools expect kids to rest lying down until nap time is over.

Safety and Security

You want to know that your child is safe and secure at preschool. All states set minimum safety and security standards, but it's a good idea to inquire about the school's policies. For instance, all students should sign in and out each day, and only authorized caregivers should be able to drop off or pick up your child. If your child is going on a field trip, the teacher should send a permission slip home for parents, and all the children should wear a school T-shirt or something that identifies them as part of the group.

Teachers should be trained in pediatric first aid and CPR, and any injuries requiring nominal first aid should be recorded on an accident sheet and reported to the parent. Classroom furniture should be clean and free of jagged edges, and all toys and indoor and outdoor play equipment should be in good condition. The playground should be fenced completely.

WHAT MATTERS MOST?

What characteristics will provide an environment your child will thrive in and learn from? Only you can decide. Ultimately, there's no such thing as the perfect preschool. You'll want to determine what you want from an ideal preschool, but then keep in mind that a program that meets all of your needs might not exist. So stay flexible and realize that you may need to compromise on some qualities to get those that are most important to you. Also, don't be surprised if your priorities change as you go through the process and you don't stick to your initial criteria. As you visit schools in person and research your options, what you thought you wanted in a school might change. Keep an open mind and trust your gut.

Every parent has to develop his or her own criteria on what is important in choosing a preschool. In addition to everything we've talked about here, for some parents, the reputation of the school matters a lot. No one can judge you for that. But always remember that your child's well-being is the most important thing, so choose a school that suits him best. The prestige of your child's preschool won't be much consolation if your child is unhappy or when you're irritated by an extra-long commute every day.

It's helpful to write down the criteria that are important to you in your child's preschool. Use the preschool comparison chart (in appendix 1) to fill in the characteristics you'd ideally like to see at your dream preschool. It will help you keep track of what's important to you as you research different programs.

In the next chapter, you'll learn about the different educational approaches and types of programs that are out there. With a little effort, you'll find the ones that are compatible with your child's and your family's needs.

CHAPTER 5

Types of Preschool Programs

MONTESSORI, PLAY BASED, COOPERATIVE—THERE ARE many different types of preschool programs out there. Whether you already know the type of teaching method you're looking for or have no clue what the differences are, it's a good idea to be familiar with the more common types of early education philosophies. You don't have to be an expert—a general understanding of the different approaches is enough to help you figure out what kind of environment is right for your child.

A nursery school's philosophy has a lot to do with the kinds of learning goals the program emphasizes, how the teacher interacts with the students, and what kind of toys and materials are available in the classroom. Each individual school may interpret a particular teaching method in its own way. Many preschools combine philosophies, taking ideas from several to create their own approach.

When reviewing the different types of schools, picture your child in each setting, keeping in mind that she'll probably do well in more than one kind of program. When reading about the different philosophies in this chapter, keep in mind that the personality traits listed for children that may do well with each philosophy are not set in stone and should be used just as a guide. As all approaches have valid points, it's up to you to decide which is right for your child and your family. Also, be sure to read each school's mission statement carefully, and talk to the director during your visit to see how he describes the school's educational philosophy.

CHILD CENTERED VERSUS TEACHER DIRECTED

All the major teaching philosophies fall into either the "child-centered" or the "teacher-directed" categories. Most preschools incorporate both child-centered and teacher-directed activities at some point in their daily curriculum.

Child Centered

In a child-centered classroom, children choose what activities they want to do and when to do them. This type of program is fairly unstructured, and children learn at their own pace, usually playing by themselves or in small groups.

Teacher Directed

Teacher-directed classrooms have a more structured feel, as teachers tell the children what activities to do and when they will do them. All of the students are expected to follow a set schedule of activities that the teacher has planned, so they all do the same thing at the same time.

PLAY BASED

The play-based philosophy, also called developmentally appropriate or progressive, is the most common preschool philosophy in the United States and falls in the "child-centered" category. The belief is that children learn best through play, so kids should be able to choose their own activities on the basis of what interests them at the time. This increases their motivation to learn and try new things, building creativity, confidence, and a love for school. Kids get to learn about a wide variety of subjects in an age-appropriate way. As each child develops at his or her own pace, teachers support and encourage students to try slightly more challenging activities when they're ready.

Teachers set up the classroom with stimulating materials and activities and facilitate learning while the children play and explore. For example, if children start exploring the sand table, the teacher may take that opportunity to ask questions that encourage them to think and investigate ("What happens if we mix sand and water?") or build their vocabulary ("What words can we use to describe wet or dry sand?").

Different stations are set up around the room—a reading corner, a dramatic play area (e.g., pretend kitchen and dress-up clothes to encourage imaginative play), a puzzle table, and so on. Lots of open-ended activities, such as blocks, a sand or water table, and art materials are available to promote creativity (as there is more than one way a child can play with them) and cooperation (because other children can easily join in). Building a block tower, for instance, teaches children concepts like shapes and sizes, balance, and cause-and-effect, as well as hand-eye coordination. By exposing children to stimulating materials and fun, age-appropriate activities, pre-reading and pre-math skills develop naturally, without the child even being aware of them.

There is a strong emphasis in play-based programs on social skills and emotional intelligence. In a play-based program, kids learn negotiating, problem solving, and decision making. They get practice asking and answering questions, following and leading, and accommodating others. One of the most important things a child can learn is how to get along with others, by sharing, taking turns, understanding others' feelings, and resolving conflicts with words instead of crying or hitting. Teachers facilitate those skills by helping kids negotiate who gets to play with a toy or what role each person gets to assume in make-believe play. This way, children will know how to make friends and get along with their peers when they reach kindergarten, where teachers focus more on math, reading, and other academic skills and less on interpersonal skills.

In a play-based program, the whole class will come together for circle time, snack time, nap time, and so on, but otherwise kids aren't expected to sit still for long periods of time. There is constant talking between teachers and students and among the kids themselves. A program may draw from other philosophies such as Reggio Emilia or Montessori or may incorporate some academic content.

Is a Play-Based School Right for Your Child?

A play-based approach is great for most children, though some may do better with more structure. If you're looking for more social and developmental growth rather than academic learning at this point in your child's life, a play-based pre-school may be right for your family. Children will probably do well in a play-based school if they

- like being active and have a lot of energy
- enjoy socializing with other kids
- aren't bothered by noisy play or lots of things going on at the same time

MONTESSORI

Dr. Maria Montessori developed her child-centered teaching method for preschool-age children in Italy in the early part of the twentieth century. It is based on her concept that play is the child's work. Although Montessori schools focus on academics, the goal is to let learning happen naturally through real-life experiences and at the child's own pace. Another important goal is to foster independence and self-esteem. Schools accomplish this by allowing children to make their own choices and by teaching them how do to things for themselves, such as putting their shoes on the right feet or pouring themselves a glass of milk.

Montessori classrooms are warm and inviting, with a calm and orderly atmosphere. Classrooms are structured around particular areas: practical life, sensorial, language, mathematics, and culture (includes geography, science, and music). Within those areas are special toys called manipulatives. Many of the manipulatives allow for self-correction, which means that they allow children to find mistakes by themselves and keep trying until they're successful. This lets them solve problems on their own and gives them greater confidence to tackle more challenging tasks. In the sensorial area, they might learn about colors by ordering wooden color tablets from lightest to darkest. A child may learn numbers in the math area by tracing rough-textured numbers and saying the number as they trace. In the practical life area, children may learn how to use buttons and zippers using manipulatives but also learn to bake bread, sweep the floor, or wash dishes (don't expect this at home). Singing, dancing, and art activities are part of the culture area. All of this is called work, although it feels like play to the children.

In the Montessori classroom, teachers serve as guides, demonstrating how to use the manipulatives and then stepping back to let the children explore on their own. Students usually work independently on floor mats or in small groups while the teacher quietly moves around the room helping and observing them. As each child gets to learn at her own pace, once the child masters a work, the teacher will introduce a more challenging one. Children also learn responsibility and respect for one another and their environment, such as putting their work away properly when they're finished with it and cleaning up after themselves during snack time. All materials are to be properly used, so a broom, for instance, can only be used for sweeping—not as a pretend rocket ship. Classrooms mix students from two and a half or three years to six years of age, which includes preschoolers and kindergartners, so older children learn to help the younger ones, and the younger kids benefit by having older peers as role models and tutors.

Montessori schools may be affiliated with either the Association Montessori Internationale (AMI) or the American

Montessori Society (AMS). The AMI schools tend to follow Maria Montessori's original teachings to the letter, whereas AMS schools are often less strict and may allow kids to play dress up, for example. Both require schools and teachers to undergo extensive accreditation programs. Schools may call themselves Montessori without being affiliated with AMS or AMI, but that doesn't necessarily mean they're not high quality. When looking at any program, you'll want to observe the classroom, ask about the curriculum, find out what kind of training the teachers have, and talk to the staff to see whether your child would be comfortable there.

> **Real Parents Talk**
>
> We really like how our children have grown under the Montessori education. At home, they're able to select a project (whether it be a puzzle, a book, a toy, or a drawing) on their own and work on it independently. When they're done, they always know that they need to put it back on the shelf where it came from. They're encouraged to take care of themselves, whether it be dressing themselves, pursuing their interests, or cleaning up after their activities.
>
> —Angela P., Seattle, Washington

Is a Montessori Preschool Right for Your Child?

If you're looking for a calm, child-centered learning environment that emphasizes academics, a Montessori school can be a wonderful option. Children may do well at a Montessori nursery preschool if they

- are independent and like playing on their own
- can follow directions
- have a long attention span

You can learn more about Montessori preschools at the following websites:

- American Montessori Society, at www.amshq.org
- Association Montessori Internationale, at www.montessori-ami.org
- The Montessori Foundation, at www.montessori.org

REGGIO EMILIA

This philosophy began in the 1940s in the Italian city of Reggio Emilia, when parents and teachers got together to find a way to improve their local schools after the end of World War II. The child-centered approach is based on the belief that children are capable, curious learners who must be free to learn for themselves and express their thoughts and ideas.

Reggio-inspired preschools follow a project-based curriculum guided by the interests of the students. If a group of children start observing and asking about birds, for example, the teacher may begin a birds project. The class may read books and sing songs about birds, create binoculars out of empty cardboard rolls for bird watching, make bird feeders, and take a field trip to a local pet store. Projects can last anywhere from a few days to a full year, and the teacher can choose to involve the group of kids or the entire class.

> **Real Parents Talk**
>
> I'm impressed with the Reggio Emilia approach and how the children lead the direction of the curriculum with the teacher's guidance. I love seeing all the documentation on the walls like the pictures and quotes from the children and all their drawings and paintings.
>
> —Ki K., Montclair, New Jersey

Children are encouraged to explore, ask questions, and hunt for the answers. This fosters their intellectual curiosity and helps to build confidence, independence, and problem-solving skills. Art is considered a valuable learning tool and incorporated into every project. In what Reggio educators refer to as "the hundred languages of children," students are encouraged to use many methods of expression to communicate and reinforce what they're learning, including music, painting, sculpture, dramatic play, storytelling, and puppetry.

Teachers actively participate in the projects and learn alongside the children, rather than sitting back and observing. When questions are posed by the children, teachers guide them toward the information rather than answering for them. Teachers also document everything that's going on in the classroom with photos, videos, written observations, and transcriptions of the students' conversations. This documentation lets kids (and their parents) revisit things they've done earlier. It shows them their own progress and that their work is important. The teachers review the documentation and reflect on what they are learning as well, about themselves and about teaching.

Under the Reggio philosophy, the environment is considered the "third teacher." A typical classroom is filled with sunlight, plants, and natural materials, and is carefully designed to support exploration and cooperation. In addition to the documentation and artwork displayed throughout the room, there are areas for small and large groups to work together, as well as common areas for children from different classrooms to interact with one another.

Parental involvement and communication is very important, as parents and teachers are viewed as partners in their child's learning experience. Many Reggio-inspired schools provide volunteer opportunities and hold educational workshops for parents, and they encourage parental participation in discussions on everything from curriculum planning to school policy.

Is a Reggio Emilia Preschool Right for Your Child?

If you're looking for a preschool that's all about following the child's natural inclination to learn, a Reggio-inspired school could be just what you're looking for. You'll also almost feel like you're there yourself when you see all the photos and other documentation the teacher collects about your child. Reggio Emilia may be right for children who

- are creative and enjoy art, dramatic play, or music
- do well in a group environment, working and playing collaboratively with other kids
- love hands-on activities and exploring

You can learn more about Reggio-inspired preschools at the following websites:

- North American Reggio Emilia Alliance, at www.reggio alliance.org
- Innovative Teacher Project, at www.innovativeteacher project.org

WALDORF

In 1919, Rudolf Steiner, an Austrian scientist and educational theorist, founded the Waldorf approach. The Waldorf philosophy is child centered but has a strong group orientation and a predictable structure and routine. For instance, Mondays may be bread-baking day and Tuesdays may be painting day, or the teacher may read the same story at story time for a week. This rhythm and predictability give students a sense of familiarity and well-being. Waldorf focuses on creativity and the arts and emphasizes cooperation and working together. Based on the idea of educating the whole child—body, mind, and spirit—Waldorf schools provide a warm, nurturing environment that feels more like a home than a school.

Waldorf nursery schools use hands-on activities and imaginary play to foster a love of learning, a sense of teamwork, and concentration skills. Teachers stimulate learning by engaging in activities that children can readily imitate, like painting and singing. Creative and dramatic play, such as arts and crafts and dress up, are strongly encouraged, as are practical activities such as cooking and gardening. Academics are not emphasized at all.

Waldorf classrooms are designed to engage children with the natural world, so they use natural materials that stimulate all five senses, like shells, rope, beeswax crayons, cloth, and wooden (never plastic) toys. There are few writing tools or books—instead there is a lot of storytelling and singing. Parents are encouraged to support the program by skipping television and computers at home. A school must be affiliated with its local Waldorf organization to use the Waldorf name and teachers must receive special training through the Association of Waldorf Schools of North America.

Is a Waldorf Preschool Right for Your Child?

If you're looking for a nurturing, homelike preschool where creativity is encouraged and academics are not emphasized, a Waldorf school can be a lovely place to go to preschool. A Waldorf preschool may be right for children who

- are comfortable playing and exploring in groups
- learn well through imitation and repetition
- are imaginative free spirits

You can learn more about Waldorf preschools at the website of the Association of Waldorf Schools of North America, at www.whywaldorfworks.org.

ACADEMIC

Also known as traditional, the academic approach is a more structured, teacher-directed approach focused on formal reading and math readiness skills, such as learning letter names and sounds and how to count. The philosophy behind the academic approach is that preschoolers benefit by preparing for the rigors of kindergarten and beyond at an early age. Similar to what children can expect to find in kindergarten, schools have a closely followed daily schedule of planned activities so that each day is consistent and predictable. Play takes place during recess outdoors or perhaps during a free-play period, but classroom time is devoted to developing skills such as identifying colors; measuring time; solving problems; and other reading, writing, and math skills. Teachers often plan a curriculum around a theme, such as farms or seasons. Traditional programs also teach classroom etiquette like raising your hand before speaking, following the teacher's instructions, and sitting in your seat until a lesson is over.

The classroom resembles those in play-based preschools

with art, blocks, reading, and other areas, but instead of kids choosing what they want to play with and how, the teacher explains and leads the activities. The teacher may ask students to color in the letter *H* or count how many circles appear on a worksheet. During a story or sing-along, the teacher might point to a picture or hold up an object and ask the class what color or shape it is. The idea is to introduce kids to the way an elementary school classroom works and to ease the transition into kindergarten and prepare them for formal learning.

Is an Academic Preschool Right for Your Child?

If you're looking for a preschool that introduces academic subjects in a structured classroom environment, an academic preschool could be the right option. Children may do well in an academic preschool if they

- are able to follow instructions
- can sit still and pay attention for twenty to thirty minutes
- do well with structure and direction

PRESCHOOL SETTINGS

Preschools following any of the approaches previously described can take place in a variety of settings. Each setting has its own characteristics, and one style may work better for your family than another.

Preschools in Child Care Centers

Some high-quality preschools are housed in child care centers, or day cares, and make a great option for working parents, in particular, who need full-day care for their kids. The differences between day-care preschool programs and other preschools are mainly in the logistics. Child care centers enroll infants from several weeks or months old to preschool-age children or older. Most are open during the full workday, five days per week (and may have a variety of schedules for parents to choose from), whereas preschools typically offer more limited hours (though extended care may be available). The preschool curriculum may take place in the morning with free play during the afternoon or throughout the day with plenty of free time mixed in. Child care centers are also open year-round and accept new children as spaces open up, whereas many preschools follow an academic school year and start with a new class each fall.

Because so many parents work full time, centers generally don't close for holidays, vacation, parent-teacher conferences, or teacher professional development days as often as other preschools, which saves parents the time and cost of finding alternative child care on those occasions. Parent involvement is usually less expected, especially during the school day, and school functions and playdates tend to be scheduled in the evenings or on weekends to accommodate working families' schedules. Some day cares also offer before- and after-school care for elementary school children, so after children leave to attend kindergarten they can still spend their nonschool hours in a familiar setting. If your child will need transportation, find out whether the day care or school provides a bus service.

Other benefits to child care centers are that, in many cases, children aren't required to be toilet trained. Teachers often even help with potty training, which can be a big stress reliever for parents. Tuition may also be less expensive on an hourly basis once you take into account the cost of extended care at other nursery schools. If your child isn't already in the day care before the age of two or three, however, it can be difficult to get into the preschool program, as most of those spots may be taken by kids moving

Real Parents Talk

We feel really lucky to have such an amazing preschool at our day care. Not only are the teachers great, but it was extremely convenient in that we didn't have to switch schools or our schedule. Plus, we've known most of the families since our kids were babies and almost all of the kids have working moms I can relate to.

—Tracy L., Philadelphia, Pennsylvania

up from the younger class. Also, if you're interested in a specific teaching approach such as Reggio Emilia or Montessori, it may be harder to find in a day-care setting, as most tend to be play based.

Because any child care center can call itself a preschool, when researching programs, you should carefully look at the facilities, teachers, and curriculum, as well as all your other preschool selection criteria. As with any high-quality preschool, trained and experienced teachers should provide age-appropriate learning activities that stimulate children's development; they should not simply watch over and play with them. Typically, it's the large centers with their own facilities that offer a nursery school curriculum for the kids in that age group, though some family day cares do as well in the caregiver's home. If, however, a center mixes infants with older children in the same room, these are generally not considered preschools.

Co-op Preschools

Co-op preschools, also known as cooperative or parent participation schools, are run by the parents. They do everything from assisting in the classroom and editing the newsletter to managing the finances and washing windows. The parents also get to decide what types of curriculum, teachers, and activities they want for their children. There is typically a paid, professional teacher who leads the classroom and sometimes also acts as the director. Otherwise, parents do everything else. For those with flexible schedules, a co-op can be a great, affordable option, as the sweat equity keeps the tuition cost much lower than at other nursery schools. Co-op preschools are usually play based and operate on a part-time schedule.

> ### Real Parents Talk
>
> We like the volunteer requirement at our co-op. We feel more in touch with what's happening in the classroom, know the teachers, students, and families really well, and get to see firsthand who she plays with and how she's developing.
>
> —Joann L., Ann Arbor, Michigan

In a co-op program, parents participate in the classroom on a regular basis, at evening meetings, on work-party days, and during off hours for projects such as fundraising or admissions. A parent may have a specific job, like arranging field trips or managing the website. Some co-ops allow a certain amount of buyout of the volunteer commitment by paying a fee, but not all programs offer this option. Most offer parent-education nights at which parents learn about topics related to early childhood development.

Many parents enjoy spending time with their child in the classroom and becoming closely involved in their child's education and daily interactions with friends. Because of all the time spent together, the families at co-op preschools often form a close-knit community. It's almost like having a new, extended family.

Religious-Affiliated Preschools

If you want your child to receive age-appropriate religious instruction in preschool, you might want to look at a school that is affiliated with a church, synagogue, or other religious organization. A religious-affiliated program might follow any of the educational philosophies or a combination of them, just like other nursery schools, but it also incorporates some degree of religious content through stories, songs, and so on.

The amount of religious instruction varies from school to school, as well as whether the program enrolls students who are not of that particular faith. Some incorporate religion as part of the daily routine; others barely mention religion. Some schools welcome students from all backgrounds and make them feel at home. Others focus more on providing religious education to children of that particular faith and give strong admissions preference to families who practice the religion or are already members of the congregation. Some even require a minimum of one or two year's membership to prevent parents from joining just to gain school admission. If you're looking for a preschool that will teach your religious beliefs and traditions, be sure to visit the school and talk to the teachers so that you understand their approach. The teachers should be trained in early childhood education principles as well as in the religion.

Bear in mind that a nursery school might be housed in a church or synagogue without actually being affiliated with it.

Some preschools were founded by a particular church but are nondenominational in practice, so don't assume that a school is religious affiliated because of its name or location. If you aren't sure, check the school's website or call to find out.

Language-Immersion and Bilingual Preschools

In bilingual and language-immersion preschools, the class is conducted partly or entirely in a foreign language. You can find nursery schools that teach French, Spanish, German, Chinese, Italian, and Japanese, among other languages. Children learn languages easily at a young age, and these programs are designed to take advantage of that window. Parents often choose a language-immersion or bilingual school because they want their children to be bilingual in a new language or in an environment that reinforces their own cultural heritage.

In a language-immersion classroom, the teacher may demonstrate what she means when speaking for the benefit of children new to the language. But the teacher rarely, if ever, translates. At a bilingual school, English and the other language may each be spoken about half the time either throughout the day or on alternate days.

In addition to language, children also learn about the cultures that speak that language and become more acquainted with the idea of a global community. The program's content may draw on other preschool teaching philosophies but be carried out in the language of choice.

If you're interested in teaching your child another language but are not ready to commit to a language-immersion or bilingual program, look for a preschool that offers children exposure to a foreign language in the curriculum. There are many programs that teach a second language through singing and storytelling or through optional after-school classes.

HOW MUCH DOES IT MATTER?

By now you may have decided that your ideal nursery school will be a full-time, play-based program with an art specialist that incorporates some Reggio Emilia teaching methods. Or you may be leaning toward a Spanish bilingual co-op program with a low teacher-student ratio. On the other hand, you might be feeling a little overwhelmed looking at all these options and wondering, "Does it really matter what type of preschool my child goes to? Is one philosophy or setting better than another?" The answer is yes and no.

Most children do well in any preschool setting, as long as it's a high-quality program in which teachers are nurturing and responsive, and kids can explore intellectually, socially, and physically. What matters right now is finding a good fit with your child's personality, your family's needs and values, and the preschool program. Let this guide your decision as you sift through all the information.

Once you have a good feeling for the kind of school you're looking for, the next step is to find preschools in your area that match your preferences.

CHAPTER 6

Researching Preschools

NOW THAT YOU'VE NARROWED DOWN your list of criteria, you can start building a list of preschools that fit your needs. Be sure to give yourself enough time to research all the programs in your area and see what each has to offer so that you can comparison shop. Preschool is an important decision to make for your child—take the time to find a great match.

There may not be one perfect program that meets all your criteria exactly, but there will be some that come close. Know your priorities but be open-minded as you do research, visit schools, and discover what each program has to offer. You may find that the characteristics you considered essential may change or that you are more flexible than you thought. It's natural for your criteria to evolve as you visit and learn more about preschools. Be sure to explore all your options, and don't limit yourself to the schools with the best reputation or where your friends' kids attend. Last, remember to take good notes and keep all your paperwork for each school organized together.

HOW TO FIND PRESCHOOLS

Word of Mouth

You can't beat word of mouth as the best way to find out about preschools in your area. Talk to your friends, neighbors, coworkers, members of your mothers' group or church, and parents you meet at the playground. Ask which preschool their kids attend and what other programs they considered and why. See the "Talk to Current Parents" section later in this chapter for other questions to ask. Your child's current day care or even your local library may also be great sources of preschool recommendations.

Keep in mind that recommendations are only one of the many valuable sources of information you have at your fingertips. There are many different types of preschools out there, and what your friends are looking for could be different from what you're trying to find for your child, so it's important to do your own research and try not to evaluate programs solely by others' comments, whether positive or negative.

Preschool Directory Websites

The online directories listed here provide local preschool searches and information on individual schools, as well as helpful articles on preschool in general. When reading parent reviews and ratings, remember that those are subjective and may be based on just a few parents' opinions.

- **Savvy Source (www.savvysource.com)** is an online directory of preschools across the country. In-depth preschool profiles are available for major cities including New York,

Los Angeles, San Francisco, Chicago, Boston, San Diego, Dallas, and Seattle.

- **GreatSchools (www.greatschools.org)** lists almost one hundred thousand public and private preschools, as well as elementary, middle, and high schools. It also has many helpful articles on schools and education.
- **NAEYC (www.naeyc.org)**, the website for the National Association for the Education of Young Children, allows you to search its database for accredited programs.

Child Care Referral Agency

There are more than seven hundred state and local child care resource and referral agencies (CCR&Rs) nationwide. Their goal is to help ensure that families all over the country have access to high-quality, affordable child care. Parents can call or stop by their local CCR&R to find licensed preschools and day cares in their area, as well as information on state licensing requirements. Search for your local CCR&R at the website of Child Care Aware (www.childcareaware.org) or call 1-800-424-2246.

Preschool Fair

If your community holds an annual preschool fair, don't miss this great one-stop-shopping opportunity. Preschool fairs are usually held by a local community organization, parents' group, or church. You can meet the directors and staff of many different schools, pick up information packets, and ask questions—all in one place. Fairs are a great way to learn more about unfamiliar programs and to gather more information on the ones you're already interested in. You can also meet current parents and hear firsthand about their child's experiences at the school. Even if you don't have time to meet everybody, you'll probably get a program or flyer with a list of all the participating preschools. Plan to arrive early, expect crowds, and try to be focused and efficient. It's probably a good idea to leave your child at home. To find a fair in your area, ask a local parents' group, or do a web search on "preschool fair" and the name of your city.

Search the Web

Sites like Yahoo! Local (http://local.yahoo.com) and Google Maps (http://maps.google.com) let you search for preschools in a specific area, just like any other business. After entering your address, search for "preschool" on Yahoo! or in Google click on "search nearby" and then enter "preschool." You'll get a list of the preschools closest to where you live. Keep in mind that this is a limited resource, and some schools might not show up, but these sites are a good starting point to find programs in your neighborhood.

You can also find general information on preschools by doing a general web search for "preschool" and your city and state. You'll not only get preschools' websites, but also you might find interesting news articles, websites, blogs, and forums about programs in your area.

Local Resources

Your community may have a local parenting magazine or websites where you can find articles about and advertisements for preschools in the area. Mothers' groups and parenting resource centers may hold workshops on finding preschools or host a preschool fair. If you're lucky, one of these resources might publish a directory that lists all of the preschools in the area.

If you live in Manhattan, Los Angeles, or San Francisco, there are published guidebooks you can find at the library or buy at a local bookstore. Not all guides are updated regularly, so keep in mind that some information (like tuition costs) might not be current.

- **New York City:** *The Manhattan Directory of Private Nursery Schools*, by Victoria Goldman
- **Los Angeles:** *The Whitney Guide: The Los Angeles Preschool Guide*, by Fiona Whitney
- **San Francisco:** *Preschools by the Bay*, by Irene Byrne

NARROWING DOWN YOUR LIST OF PRESCHOOLS

After doing everything in the previous section, you should be ready to start making some comparisons. The following sections will help you pare your list of schools down and determine which programs to apply to.

Check Out the Preschool's Website

Most preschools today have a website. This will probably be your best introduction to the progam. They typically provide basic information about the school's philosophy, location, tuition, schedule, age requirements, and staff. Some go into greater detail and cover the admissions procedure, financial aid, daily curriculum, statistics about the student body, and policies on things like discipline, toilet training, and meals. A few allow you to download application forms and schedule tours online. School websites that provide information on current events like family picnics and fundraising events can give you a sense of what the community is like. Keep in mind that not all preschools update their website regularly, so check to see that the dates and other information are current.

Call the Preschool

Once you have a good idea of the preschools you're interested in, call them up! Ask them to mail a brochure and an application to you. Get information about the program, operating hours, tuition, registration policy, and other essentials you don't already have. Be sure to ask any other critical questions you have that would make or break your decision to visit the school (see chapter 7 for a list of potential questions). Finally, make an appointment to see the school in person.

Each school has its own admissions process, so make sure you understand exactly what it is and what you need to do by when. If anything in the process doesn't seem clear, now's the time to ask. If it's a selective program, you should also ask questions that will help you gauge your child's chances of being admitted, such as the following:

- How many openings are there for children of my child's age?
- How many of those spots do you expect siblings to take?
- How many applicants do you expect?
- What are the criteria for admission?
- If the school has a waiting list, how long is the wait? If I apply now, what are the chances of my child being admitted in the month and year I'm looking for?

Plan a School Visit

Visiting preschools is probably the most critical part of your research, so it's important to make room in your schedule to go. Try to visit more than a few places, as not all will make your short list, and add to those if you're looking at programs that are difficult to get in. Most preschools offer tours and open houses or allow you to visit with your child and observe. Going during school hours is your best option so that you can see how the class works and how teachers interact with the children. See chapter 7 for useful advice on what to look for and questions to ask during the visit.

Talk to Current Parents

You might know parents whose kids currently attend the preschool. If not, ask your friends if they do, or strike up a conversation with a parent during a school visit. You could also ask the school for the names of any parents who have volunteered to discuss the program with potential families. Current parents are a great source of information. Ask them about their opinions of the school and its strengths and weaknesses, and how they feel about the teachers. Find out about the little things on your mind that aren't on the website but that you don't want to bother school officials with, like how easy it is to find a place to park in the morning or what classes the after-school program offers.

Good questions to ask include the following:

- Why did you choose this preschool for your child?
- How do parents feel about the teachers and director?
- What do you like most about the school?

- What does your child like best about school?
- Did anything surprise you about the school after your child started there?
- Is there anything you wish you could change about the school?

HOW MANY PRESCHOOLS SHOULD YOU APPLY TO?

There is no magic number of preschools you should apply to. If you're willing to pay all those application fees, you could apply to dozens. But if you've taken the time to research your options carefully, you'll be able to whittle your list down to a manageable handful of programs.

If the programs you're considering are somewhat selective such that there's no guarantee of getting a spot, applying to four to six schools is a reasonable goal. Of course, the number of applications you finally submit will depend on several factors:

- **When are you applying?** If your child is very young and you're getting on waiting lists well in advance, you'll be making your choices on the basis of what's important to you at the time. A lot can happen in the subsequent year or two. At that point, you'll better understand your child's personality and your own scheduling, location, and other needs. So don't hesitate to get on wait lists for any preschools you find interesting, but allow room for things to change as time goes on.
- **What are your chances at the preschools you like?** If some of the schools are extremely popular, have few spaces available, or give preference to a group you don't belong to (such as members of a church), be prepared to apply to a larger number of schools. But do apply to all the ones

you're interested in, even if they seem hard to get into. You never know until you try.

- **What are the admissions processes at your potential preschools?** How much time can you devote to the process? The more schools you apply to, the less time you'll have to spend on each application. If you'll be writing parent statements and attending child and parent interviews (usually held on weekdays) for several schools, plan accordingly so you put in your best effort for each school.

- **How much are you willing or able to spend on application fees?** Application fees can be as low as $10 or as much as $100 or more, so the process can be very expensive if you apply to a lot of schools. Don't let that stop you from applying, but you might want to think twice about paying a fee for a school you're not that interested in.

In appendix 1, you'll find a preschool comparison chart to help you compare programs side by side and against the criteria you established in chapters 3 and 4; appendix 2 includes a preschool profile form that you can photocopy and use to help keep track of each program's information and your observations. You can also re-create the documents on an electronic spreadsheet with the schools as columns and the profile items as rows.

CHAPTER 7

Visiting Preschools

BY NOW YOU'VE NARROWED DOWN your choices to several preschools. You've thumbed through the brochures and perused the websites. You've read the school's mission statement and looked at the photos of children grinning from ear to ear and engaging in fun activities in beautiful classrooms. But beyond the pictures, what is the preschool really like?

Before spending time and money on applications, you should make every effort to visit the programs you're interested in. This will give you a chance to meet the teachers and see them in action in the classroom, tour the facilities, and talk face-to-face with the staff and parents of current students. Seeing the actual environment will help you get a better understanding of the program, the school's approach to teaching, and its strengths and weaknesses. Most important of all, the visit will help you decide if a particular preschool is the right place for your child.

DECIDING WHICH PRESCHOOLS TO VISIT

No matter how certain you are about what you're looking for in a preschool, you're probably curious about different types of programs and educational approaches. If so, go ahead and visit a range of preschools. You'll get to observe various philosophies practiced in the classroom and see how two preschools following the same approach may be completely different from each other because of other factors.

You might feel strongly that your introverted child needs a small class size. But on visiting more schools, you might discover a school with a larger class but a nurturing teacher who pays careful attention to each child's needs. You might think your very active child needs a lot of structure to learn to focus and follow directions, only to discover she fits best in a classroom that lets her choose what she wants to play with. You might have planned to send your child to a French-immersion, play-based school, but she had such a great interaction with the teacher at an English-speaking Montessori program that you decide to apply there and sign her up for a weekly French class instead.

Keep in mind that the more places you visit, the better you'll understand your own priorities. Seeing schools in person will give you a much clearer understanding of what aspects you like about a program and the ones that won't work for your family. You'll also figure out which questions to ask and what to look for when you observe a classroom.

> **Real Parents Talk**
>
> Originally, I pictured our twins in a small, church-based nursery school, but when I saw how much they enjoyed being in a big, busy classroom and climbing the huge outdoor structure, we decided to go with a larger preschool setting instead.
>
> —Elaine H., Woodbridge, New Jersey

OPPORTUNITIES TO VISIT

Typically, parents are able to visit a preschool by taking a tour, attending an open house, or making a private appointment.

Preschool Tour

A tour is the most common way for parents to visit preschools. You get to see the facilities, meet the staff, learn more about the program, and mingle with other prospective parents. The school's director, another member of the staff, or a volunteer parent might conduct the tour. If school is in session, you'll stop by the classroom for a few minutes and see how the teachers interact with the kids and how the kids work with one another. Tours may be available for individual families or small groups. Each school will let you know its policy about bringing your child with you.

Open House or Information Session

Open houses or information sessions are usually held in the evenings or on weekends for prospective parents. The purpose is to give a general overview of the program, usually with presentations from the director and teachers. There may also be a group tour of the school grounds.

Although open houses can be great sources of information, they attract a large number of parents. So there isn't much opportunity to ask questions or get to know the staff, and you won't see the classroom dynamics. If you have the option of an open house or a tour, take the tour. If you can do both, that's even better.

Some schools hold more informal open houses during school hours and welcome both parents and children. These typically last a few hours, and families get to spend some time playing in the classroom, chatting with teachers, and hearing about the program from current parents. A formal information session and tour of the school grounds might also be incorporated.

Real Parents Talk

January is preschool open house season where we live. We had to take time off work and spend weekends and evenings going to them, but it was worth it. They not only gave us a good sense for the programs, but we also got a chance to talk to other parents checking out schools and find out the scoop on other places. One of the mothers I met during a visit told me to look at the preschool next door because she thought it was far better, and she was right. That's where we ended up enrolling.

—Paula C., Palo Alto, California

Classroom Visit

Some preschools allow parents to visit on their own and observe a class. Call the school to ask whether it's possible to schedule an appointment to do this, and ask when the best time would be. You'll learn more by visiting during indoor time than outdoor time. Free-play period is a particularly good choice because you can see the teacher working with individual students and the kinds of activities the children have to choose from.

Although you may be tempted to drop by unannounced, this can be disruptive to the classroom. It is difficult to accommodate all the prospective parents who want to wander in on top of the children and any current parents who may be there as well. Be courteous and call ahead for an appointment. This will ensure that you'll come at a time when the director can talk with you and the class can be observed. You won't see much if the kids are napping or on a field trip.

A PRIVATE VISIT COULD BE AN ADMISSIONS INTERVIEW

Even if a school doesn't schedule formal parent or child interviews as part of the admissions process, keep in mind that there are some situations in which you may not even know you're being interviewed! If the school invites you and your child for a private visit, for example, and then when you arrive the director asks you to sit down and chat while a teacher starts observing or playing with your child in the classroom, you should consider it an interview. What appears to be a casual conversation may be a chance for the preschool director to find out how interested you are in the program or if your child is developmentally ready for preschool. Even if he's not evaluating you, talking to the director one-on-one is still a great opportunity for you to tell him why the school is a good match for your family or how you might be able to contribute to the school community. So if a school asks you to come in for a private family visit, read chapter 10 to prepare yourself (just in case).

ARRANGING THE VISIT

Remember that each preschool's process is unique, and that includes school visits. Many schools reserve visits for parents whose children are eligible to enroll for the upcoming school year. Others allow any families to schedule a visit, regardless of the child's age. Some ask that only parents attend, while others require the child to come along. In some cases, parents are required to go to an open house or on a tour just to receive an application form.

Here are a few tips for arranging your preschool visits.

- **Make your appointment as soon as possible.** Open houses and group tours that take place on set dates, as well as private appointment slots, can fill up quickly. Ask if your child should accompany you, and if so, make sure the visit isn't scheduled during her usual nap time.
- **Find a time when both parents can visit.** It's usually not required, but it's better if both of you can go (even if on separate visits) to see the school for yourselves. Visiting together also lets you take turns observing and listening to the tour guide.
- **Visit when school is in session, if possible.** You'll be able to see teachers and students interacting in the classroom.
- **Try to schedule your favorite preschools last.** Once you've visited a few places, you'll have a much better idea of what you like and don't like and which questions you want to ask. Seeing your top-choice preschools last will put you in the best position to compare them with others on your list.

WHAT IF YOU CAN'T VISIT?

You may be in a situation where you can't visit preschools in person, perhaps because you live in another state and are planning to relocate to the area or because of other commitments. Although nothing can replace an in-person visit, there are other ways to "see" the school without actually setting foot there. As mentioned in chapter 6, check out the school's website, read parent reviews on the online preschool directory sites, and call the school and ask a lot of questions (see the list at the end of this chapter for ideas). If the school's handbook or newsletters are not published online, ask for copies to read to get a sense of the policies, activities, and the community. Contact current parents for feedback from people who really know the school. Ask them to describe the classrooms and facilities and their impressions when they first visited the school.

If the tour or admissions interview is mandatory for applying, talk to the director. The school may be flexible about waiving the tour requirement if you live out of the area or let you visit when you are in town, even if it's not a regularly scheduled tour date. For a parent interview, ask if you can do it over the phone. But if the preschool is fairly competitive, you'll want to make every effort to have a face-to-face meeting (particularly if a child interview is required) so that your child is on a level playing field when it comes time for the committee to decide who gets in.

PREPARING FOR YOUR VISIT

The following sections present tips for preparing for the preschool visit.

Read about the Preschool before the Visit

If you've read the brochure and perused the website, then you won't need to ask questions that are already answered there. You're visiting to get a feel for the place, not for that kind of basic information. Spend your time looking around and asking questions that help you gather new information. At selective preschools (especially those that don't hold admissions interviews for parents), try to engage in conversation with the director (or admissions director, if there is one), and show that you're interested and knowledgeable about the program.

Arrange for Child Care

If the visit doesn't include children, or if you need child care for your other kids while you're gone, book a reliable baby-sitter. It's probably fine to bring a baby in a carrier, but always ask first. If bringing your child is optional, then it's your choice. It might be nice to be able to see how she responds to the school environment, but it will also make it harder to observe and listen to what's being said. If your child is usually fussy or needs her nap during that time of the day, it's probably better not to bring her along.

Prepare Your Questions

Jot down a list of all the questions you want to ask based on the criteria you've already established for choosing a pre-school. See the list of questions at the end of this chapter for suggestions. Go over the questions with your spouse or partner ahead of time so that he or she can pay attention for answers, too.

What to Wear

There's no need to dress up for a school visit, especially if it's a group tour or an open house. Comfortable shoes are recommended in case you'll be walking a lot or going up and down stairs, but otherwise try not to stress about your outfit. If your child accompanies you, don't dress her up in anything too fancy or uncomfortable to play in. Play clothes are fine.

If you're worried about your attire, a good rule of thumb is to dress appropriately for the school atmosphere. Jeans are probably fine at a creative, play-based nursery school but perhaps less expected at a private preschool where students wear uniforms.

DURING YOUR VISIT

The preschool visit will be your first (and perhaps only) chance to see the school in person and meet the director and staff. Be polite and pay attention to the staff members who are giving presentations and leading the tour. The next sections go over some things to pay attention to and questions to ask yourself on the school visit.

Physical Space and Materials

Look around the building and the outdoor area. Check carefully that the preschool has clean, comfortable, and safe facilities. If your child is with you, hold her hand and try not to let her play in the classroom unless the teacher invites her to.

What Is the Look and Feel of the School?

Is the atmosphere warm and inviting or cold and institutional? Is it bright and cheerful or dark and drab? What's hanging on the walls? Seasonal decorations? A large calendar with birthdays and activities? Photos or samples of the kids' artwork? Things should be hung at a child's eye level. A picture is worth a thousand words: children's original artwork shows that the school encourages creativity and imagination. Children should not be told to all draw the exact same rainbow, for example.

Is the Classroom Clean, Well Lit, and Safe?

Furniture (e.g., tables, chairs, shelves, cubbies) should be the right size for children. Is there enough space for kids to move from one activity to another without bumping into one another? Toys and materials should be appropriate for the age group and in good condition. Bathrooms should have toilets and sinks at the right height for children and should be open to the teacher's view for safety. If there are classroom pets, are they kept hygienically in a cage or aquarium? Child-safe windows should be large enough to provide plenty of natural light and a view of outdoors.

Does the Classroom Foster Learning and Interaction among Children?

You should see several centers for different activities, such as art, block play, dramatic play, and a reading corner. Are there tables where kids can work on individual or small group activities, like playing with play dough? Materials should be housed on easy-to-reach shelves that kids can get out for themselves. You should see things labeled with pictures and words throughout the classroom to help kids make a connection between spoken and written words, as well as making it easy for them to clean up so they can see where each toy belongs.

Is the Playground Stimulating and Well Maintained?

Children need plenty of space to run around, to safely expend their energy, to get exercise, and to play and socialize with their peers. A preschool playground should have equipment for climbing, swinging, and jumping, as well as a shady area where kids can play when it's hot outside. It's great to find a riding area for tricycles and scooters. If you live in a place where weather might keep kids inside for part of the year, look for a large classroom or play area where they can run and exercise indoors. It's not a good sign if the equipment seems dirty or dingy or if anything is broken.

Teachers and Children

Pay attention to the teachers and children. Do they seem happy? Do they interact in a caring and respectful way? Is this type of setting one in which your child will thrive?

Do the Children Seem Happy and Engaged?

Do the students seem happy to be there, or bored or tense? Children should be engaged in meaningful play, not wandering aimlessly or just sitting by themselves for a long time. They should be talking and learning in a normal indoor voice, with occasional loud bursts of excitement. Although classrooms shouldn't be absolutely silent, a very noisy, chaotic environment might mean the teachers aren't providing enough supervision.

Do the Teachers Seem to Enjoy Their Work?

How do the teachers interact with the students? Do they seem like they enjoy working with the children? They shouldn't seem bored or busy doing "teacher things" that take their attention away from the class. Are interactions between teachers and students warm, caring, and respectful? Do the teachers sit with children and work with them, or do they supervise from afar? Good teachers will talk with children instead of to them, asking them questions and patiently answering theirs. They should divide their time among working with individual children, small groups, and the whole group, yet always be observant of all the students in the classroom. Chances are, if you like the teachers and the children in the class seem happy, your child will like being there, too.

General Observations

In addition to the specifics of classroom and other facilities, consider the following issues as well.

Can You Picture Your Child at This Preschool?

Try to see the program from your child's perspective and consider whether she'll do well there. For instance, if the classroom is calm with children working independently, but your child likes to chatter and play with others, consider whether the setting would be a calming influence on her or make her feel constrained. Look for students in the classroom who seem similar to your child and try to imagine how happy your child would be there. If you bring your child on the visit, does she seem comfortable there? Does the teacher talk to her with kindness and respect?

What Are Other Parents Like?

Look around and meet the current preschool parents. (You'll also meet other prospective parents, but keep in mind they may not be reflective of the actual parent body.) Are they interesting and friendly? Do they seem similar to you or are they very different? Do you feel comfortable around them and think you'd get along? How do they interact with one another? Does everyone socialize with one another, or does it appear cliquey? Remember, you'll be spending a lot of time with these people in the next few years, so consider how you'll feel about spending time with them at school functions and birthday parties.

What Does Your Gut Say?

Of all the things you should take in during your visit, perhaps the most important should be the feel of the school. Even if the preschool is only two blocks from home and has a shiny, new building, if it doesn't feel right to you, then it isn't. It's critical for you to be comfortable with the teachers and the director for your child to feel happy and secure at her new school. This will be her second home and these are the people who will be your partners in her early education. You know your own child best, and only you can decide if the preschool is the right fit. You want to feel good about dropping her off there every day, knowing that's she's going to be well cared for.

What Questions Should You Ask?

The school visit is a great time to ask questions about the program and its curriculum, policies, and so on. The following section includes a list of sample questions to ask your tour guide or the preschool director. Since you'll have a limited amount of time, see if you can find information on the school's website ahead of time. Then during the visit, mention the topics that matter most to you. If current preschool parents will be at the tour, also refer to the questions back in chapter 6 in the "Talk to Current Parents" section. Review your criteria from chapters 3 and 4 to come up with any others that apply to your own situation.

When speaking to the director and admissions staff, be pleasant and respectful—you don't want to seem like you're giving them the third degree or appear to be a potential problem parent. Particularly at selective preschools, try to phrase questions in a positive way so they don't come across as criticism of the program. For instance, "How involved is the parent community?" is better than "Do all the parents have to volunteer?" Open-ended, "what if" questions will also elicit more helpful answers than yes or no ones.

QUESTIONS TO ASK DURING PRESCHOOL VISITS

Overall Program

1. Is the program licensed by the state? Do you have NAEYC accreditation?
2. Do you have an idea of how many openings will be available? How about after siblings are accounted for?

3. Are there usually enough spots for everyone who wishes to register? If not, is there a waiting list? How long does it generally take to get off the waiting list? Do you admit students on a first-come, first-served basis?

4. Do you enroll children only in the fall or whenever a space becomes available?

5. What is the price of tuition? Are there other fees for extended care, supplies, field trips, or late pickup? How often does tuition go up and by how much, on average?

6. Does the school offer financial aid for eligible families? How do you apply?

7. What is the cutoff date for new students?

8. What are the regular school hours? Is the preschool an all-day program, a half-day program, or are there several options?

9. How long is the school year? What is the vacation and holiday schedule? On what other days is the school closed? Are there any alternative arrangements available for child care when school is closed?

10. Does the school offer extended hours before and after school? What are the hours, and how much does it cost? How much advance notice is required? Who supervises the children, and what's the routine?

11. Are enrichment classes available after school? What type of classes? Is there an additional fee?

12. Is there a summer program? How does it differ from the regular program? If the school is year-round, do families have the option of going to a different summer program and reenrolling in the fall?

13. How does drop-off work? Is there curbside drop-off and pickup? Are there dedicated parking spaces for drop-off

and pickup? Does the school help arrange carpools or provide bus service?

14. If the school is attached to an elementary school, are preschoolers automatically accepted into the kindergarten? If not, what is the admissions process for kindergarten?

15. Do siblings (or children of alumni) receive preference for admission? Does that apply only if the older sibling is currently enrolled? Is there a tuition discount for siblings? Do kids get assigned to the same teacher their older sibling had? Are twins placed in the same classroom?

16. After preschool, where do your graduates go to elementary school? Does the preschool help parents applying to private schools with the kindergarten application process?

17. Is there an option for children to stay for an additional prekindergarten year if necessary? If so, do the children stay in the same classroom or is there a separate transitional kindergarten class?

18. How does the school handle children with learning differences or special needs?

Curriculum

1. How would you describe your educational philosophy? What are the advantages of this approach? How is it reflected in the curriculum?

2. How many classes are there? How many children are in each class?

3. How are the children grouped in the classroom? By age, mixed ages, or developmentally?

4. What is a typical day like? Can I see the daily schedule?

5. Are there any specialists who come in for music, art, physical education, or other activities? Do all children participate or only those who choose to join in?

6. How much of the curriculum is devoted to social and emotional development and how much to academic learning? How do the children learn letters, numbers, shapes, and colors?

7. Can kids choose their own activities, or do they follow the teacher's plan? How much of the day do they spend working independently versus in a group?

8. What happens if a child doesn't want to participate in a group activity, like circle time?

9. Do you talk about different cultures as part of the curriculum? Which holidays do you celebrate in the classroom?

10. How much time do kids spend outdoors each day?

11. Does the school take field trips? Do the teachers take children on neighborhood walks? Where and how often? How are they supervised? What safety precautions are taken? Who drives?

Teachers and Staff

1. How long has the present director been there? What is his or her background? How well does the director know the students and their families? How accessible is the director to the parents?

2. How many teachers are assigned to each classroom? How many are teachers, and how many are teacher assistants?

3. What is the teacher-student ratio? Is this ratio maintained all day?

4. What are the teachers' credentials and training? Are they certified in early childhood education? Do they receive ongoing training? How long have they been teaching preschoolers?

5. How long have the teachers been working in the school? What is the turnover rate?

6. How do you screen teachers and other staff? Do you perform background checks before hiring?

7. If a teacher is absent, do you place a substitute teacher in the classroom?

8. How would the teacher respond if there were two needy children at the same time? If one kid in the class was being disruptive in the classroom?

Home–School Connection

1. Where do most of the families live? Are there many families where both parents work? Or single-parent families?

2. How do teachers and staff communicate with parents? Do teachers have email? Is there a newsletter?

3. How do parents contact the teacher or director with questions or concerns?

4. How often do you hold parent-teacher conferences?

5. Are written progress reports sent home? How often?

6. Is there an open-door policy for parents? Can parents stop by the classroom any time to observe?

7. How can parents get involved in the preschool program? Is there a parent-teacher organization? Are meetings scheduled to accommodate working parents? Is child care provided?

8. Do parents help in the classroom or participate in class activities? Are parents required to volunteer a certain number of hours? Is there an option to pay a fee to waive the volunteer commitment?

9. How close is the parent community? What opportunities are there for parents to get to know one another? Does the school hold social events for parents, with and without kids?

10. Does the school provide contact information for the other families in the class?

Health and Safety

1. How does the school handle separation (or what is the phase-in schedule) at the beginning of the year?

2. Can parents stay in the classroom if their child is having a tough time during morning drop-off? For how long? How do teachers handle crying children (do they comfort them, redirect them to an activity, or leave them to calm themselves down)?

3. Are the teachers and staff trained in pediatric first aid and CPR?

4. Do kids have to be potty trained before enrolling? If not, does staff help with potty training? What happens if a child has an accident?

5. Is there a scheduled time when all the children go to the bathroom? If so, will the teacher take a child that needs to go at another time?

6. How does the school handle discipline? Is there a consistent policy everyone follows or do teachers handle

situations in their own way? What would happen, for instance, if a child bites a classmate or throws a tantrum?

7. What is the nap schedule (what time and for how long)? What do they sleep on? Can kids bring a stuffed toy for their nap? Do kids have to sleep or rest lying down until nap time is over? Can they read or play quietly if they can't sleep?

8. What are the food guidelines? Does the school provide lunch and/or snack, or do kids bring their own lunch? If meals are included, is the cost included in the tuition? If there is a fee, how much is it and how far in advance do you need to order? Are the meals nutritious, organic, or peanut free?

9. Are there any food restrictions? Will I be informed of how much my child eats? Is there a refrigerator or microwave in the classroom?

10. What is the preschool's sick child policy? When should a child stay home from school? What happens if a child gets sick or injured at school? Is the parent always notified if an incident occurs?

11. Are the toys and materials washed or disinfected on a regular basis? How quickly are they replaced if they break?

12. Is there an emergency plan for children that have severe allergic reactions (to food, drugs, or insect stings)?

13. Do parents or caregivers have to sign in and out during drop-off and pickup? Do you require parental permission and proper identification for someone else to pick up the child?

14. What kind of security measures do you have? How are visitors admitted? How do you monitor children on the

playground? Are the entrances and exits on the school grounds secure?

15. Is there a clearly defined emergency plan in case of a medical emergency, fire, earthquake, or tornado?

AFTER YOUR VISIT

Following your preschool visit, there are some things you'll want to take care of as soon as possible.

- **Write down your impressions, likes, and dislikes.** Be sure to do this while the visit is still fresh in your mind. Note any points that make the school stand out, names of the people you met, and any new information you learned. After a few school visits, things start to run together in your mind. If you make your notes while your memory is still fresh, you'll know which school has the once-a-week music specialist and which one has the garden tended by the students.

- **Review your list of questions.** Is there anything you forgot to ask? You can always call the school for answers. Also, jot down any new questions that you want to add for the next preschool visit.

- **Send a thank-you note to the director or tour guide.** It's a good idea to send a thank-you note, especially if your tour guide was a staff member and you had a long conversation or were given a private tour. Although sending a note isn't necessary or expected, it's a nice gesture that will be appreciated. A few sentences are just fine: say thanks for the tour, mention something specific you liked or learned about the school from the visit, and close by saying the tour confirmed the school is a great fit for your family or you know your child would be very happy there.

Here's a sample thank-you note. Of course, you'll want to customize it to fit your own style and each visit.

SAMPLE THANK-YOU NOTE

Dear Aimee,

Thank you so much for giving us the tour yesterday. It was great to see how engaged the teachers are with the children, and we especially enjoyed seeing how excited the kids were cooking applesauce in the classroom. We can certainly see why other parents describe Country Day Preschool as a "home away from home" and think Luke would really thrive in such a warm and enriching environment.

Sincerely,

Karen and Matthew Gerber

CHAPTER 8

The Preschool Admissions Process

AFTER ALL YOUR RESEARCH AND visits, you've come up with your target list of preschools. If none of them is selective, and you can enroll at any place you choose, consider yourself lucky and skip over to chapter 11 if you're still deciding or chapter 12 if you've made your decision. Otherwise, it's time to enter the admissions process.

There are two types of selective preschools. Some schools allow anyone to sign up but have more applicants than spots available. The admissions procedures for such programs are fairly straightforward (though not as much as you would think) and generally fall into one of three categories: open enrollment, waiting list, and lottery system. Other nursery schools, typically private ones, admit students using a regular admissions process (similar to college admissions), which involves an admissions committee selecting children on the basis of a number of application requirements, such as application questions and interviews.

In either case, you can increase your child's chances of

being accepted simply by understanding how the admissions process works at the preschools you're applying to. This chapter will give you insight into the different procedures, how preschools decide who gets in, and tips for upping your odds of admission.

OPEN ENROLLMENT

Preschools that use an open enrollment process begin accepting applications on a given date, typically several months prior to the September you want to enroll. Some programs admit students strictly on a first-come, first-served basis until the class is filled. So as long as you register while there are still spaces available, your child is guaranteed a space. At highly popular programs, parents have been known to line up outside very early in the morning or even camp out the night before the first day of registration to secure a spot (concert tickets, anyone?). If you find yourself in this situation, leave your child at home if possible and don't forget to bring any documents you need to register, such as your child's birth certificate or immunization records. Try to make the most of the situation by getting to know the other parents in line. After all, chances are your kids will be in the same class!

Other open enrollment schools are pickier, and after accepting applications during a set time period (between January 5 and February 12, for example), instead of first-come, first served, they select which kids will make up the class. These programs typically try to balance the number of girls and boys and ages of the students, among other things (see "How Do Preschools Decide Who Gets In?" later in this chapter to learn more).

Schools that have an open enrollment policy tend to

- accept applications during an open enrollment period, usually at the beginning of the target year
- either accept kids in the order the applications were received or select students from the application pool to create a balanced classroom (all other applications are placed on a waiting list)
- use a simple, straightforward application form.

THE WAITING LIST

Many nursery schools with waiting lists will let you send in your application any time after your child is born, but a few schools and all day cares will actually allow you to apply while you're still pregnant. Admission at these schools is primarily based on the order in which the application was received, so it pays to research preschools as early as possible to get your child a good spot on the list. That said, many programs factor in other criteria when determining which applicants are offered open positions. For instance, an open spot might go to the next child on the list with similar qualities to the student who just left (like a girl born in July,

> **Real Parents Talk**
>
> The schools we visited all said enrollment was based on a first-come, first-served basis, but in reality that didn't seem to be the case. It is also about being top of mind, making sure your application is flagged by repeated (though not annoying) efforts by the parents to keep their kid at the forefront of the director's mind. We didn't resort to writing letters like some of our friends, but we did do our share of calling!
>
> —Leon S., Mountain View, California

for instance) to keep the class balanced. Or acceptance might go to the next child in a special category, like a sibling or child of a school staff member. As parents, how often you follow up with the school and how committed you are to taking a spot if offered can also play a major role in getting off the list.

If there are a lot more applications than available spots, people who sign up too late may have little to no chance of acceptance. What's too late? It depends on the school and the length of the waiting list. At some programs, you can sign up a few weeks before your child will begin school and have no problem getting in. More competitive schools, however, may encourage you to apply while your child is still younger than a year old! If you're interested in any of these programs, don't delay submitting your application.

Once families are notified, they may be asked to visit the school and perhaps attend a family interview with the director or other staff member before enrolling. This isn't usually to evaluate you or your child, but it's a chance for the preschool to get to know your family and for you to observe the classroom and confirm that your child will attend. Unless there's a really significant reason that the school can't support your child's needs, he will generally be accepted.

Preschools with waiting lists tend to

- accept applications as soon as the child is born, or even sooner
- accept kids on a first-come, first-served basis, making exceptions to create a balanced classroom
- have a simple admissions process, usually just a straightforward application form

Year-Round Programs

Preschools that run year-round generally use a rolling admissions process, which means that kids may be offered a spot at any time during the year as spots open up (once they pass the cutoff age). Parents may get only a few weeks' notice when a space is opening and must make the decision

to enroll their child within a few days or risk losing the spot. Oftentimes, schools can tell a large number of parents in the spring that there will be a space for their child in September, as that's when they know how many kids will transfer to a different nursery school or leave for kindergarten.

Day-care centers work this way, except the cutoff age may be as young as six weeks. However, at child care centers in high demand, waiting lists can be so long that it might take two or three years to get a spot. For those who apply intending to send their child only to the preschool program, that's fine. Unfortunately, it's not so great if you need child care before then.

If a year-round school offers a spot but you're not ready to enroll your child, you can decline it and ask to continue on the waiting list. But before taking that option, find out whether that means your child will move to the *bottom* of the list and how long it might take before you're offered another spot.

Academic-Year Programs

A preschool with a traditional September-to-June school year that uses a waiting list will also let you apply when your child is very young. You won't learn if your child is accepted, wait-listed, or did not receive a spot until the school notifies you a few months before the school year starts, however.

TIPS FOR GETTING OFF THE WAITING LIST

Waiting lists are usually prioritized by the date the application was received. However, many nursery schools also try for a balance of ages and sexes, which can affect priority. For example, even if your child is number 22 on the list, he might get the next spot if the school is looking for a three-year-old boy born in the summer that can enroll in the afternoon program.

Many parents don't realize that showing a genuine interest in the school or knowing someone connected to the school can make a difference. Most schools give priority to applicants who are serious about accepting a spot. It's also more efficient to call a family who the school knows is eager to enroll than go down the list, through refusal after refusal, to get to that same family. Show your interest by speaking to the director on the tour, asking questions, and following up with him to keep your child and family fresh in his mind. Some parents send a short cover letter along with the application emphasizing their interest in the program and why it's a good fit for their child. If you have a friend or acquaintance whose child currently attends the school, ask him or her to mention your child's application to the school.

· **One to two weeks after submitting your application, call to confirm that your paperwork was received.** Ask if there's any additional information you can provide, and ask any remaining questions you may have. For rolling admissions, inquire when a space might be available. If it's an academic-year program, ask about your child's chances of getting a spot for the year he would enroll.

· **Six to ten months before you want your child to start, call the school every month or every other month to follow up on your status.** The longer the waiting list, the earlier you should call. Don't be a nuisance, just pleasantly persistent. Don't be discouraged by the length of the waiting list or let that keep you from applying. Many people on the list choose a different school, move away, or change their minds for other reasons. Your child's birth date might end up being an asset, or there may be something unique about your family that gives you higher priority. Or your clear enthusiasm for the school may pay off with a space in the class.

REGULAR ADMISSIONS

Preschools that select children on the basis of a number of subjective criteria, such as the application questions, sometimes a parent statement, and perhaps a child or parent interview, use the regular, or rounds, admissions policy. Demonstrated interest in the program and enthusiasm for its educational philosophy are always important. These schools are typically private nursery schools that follow an academic-year calendar.

Applications are typically due by a set deadline, usually between December and February prior to the September start date. A few schools review applications on a first-come, first-served basis, so it's to your advantage to submit the application as soon as possible before the class is filled. Most admissions committees, however, wait until after the application deadline to review all the applications. Families are generally notified in the spring, usually between February and April, if the child has been admitted, rejected, or placed on the waiting list (also known as the wait pool).

Wait-listed candidates are considered over the summer or during the school year as spaces open up. These lists are generally not ranked (i.e., not first-come, first-served). Schools accept children from the wait list if they meet the criteria of the spot the school needs to fill (for instance, a four-year-old girl who can enroll in the afternoon program). Schools that accept second-round applications that arrive after the initial deadline will consider those applicants for spaces that are left open after the accepted families from the first round respond.

Schools with a regular admissions process tend to

- accept applications by a certain deadline approximately six to nine months before the September start date
- select applicants on the basis of a number of criteria an admissions committee evaluates
- have applications that range in complexity from a one-page form to a multiple-page form, a parent statement, and interviews for both parents and child

LOTTERY SYSTEM

Some preschools use a lottery system to at least partly randomize the way children are selected for the incoming class. Here's how it works: Kids are randomly assigned a lottery number and then accepted in the order their number is drawn. A class may be put together by reserving a certain number of slots for various categories, such as age, sex, members and nonmembers of an affiliated organization, and any other criteria the school establishes. The remaining names are kept on a waiting list and families are notified of open spaces in the order of their lottery draw.

Schools with lottery systems tend to

- accept applications and hold the lottery during the fall or winter before the target school year
- break the lottery into groups determined by the school and stop accepting more in that category when the number of reserved slots is filled
- use a straightforward application, usually a one-page form of family and child information

DOUBLE TROUBLE: APPLYING FOR TWINS

If you have twins or other multiples, you'll need to submit a separate application for each child. Bear in mind that only one might be accepted, especially at selective schools with few slots. In this scenario, a sibling preference policy could help the second child get in the following year. For programs with waiting lists or open enrollment, you have a much better chance of both being admitted assuming you signed both up early.

So if you're looking for two spots in the same school, it's wise to apply to more than just a handful of schools. Completing five to ten preschool applications is a good idea, depending on how competitive the preschools are in your area.

There are clearly benefits to putting your twins in the same school—convenience not being the least important. But some parents choose to send twins to different programs. Maybe they have different learning styles (one does better with structure, the other with independence). It can also be an opportunity for twins to get to know other friends beyond each other. Be sure you've thought about what's important to you. Do you feel strongly that they should stay together? Would two different preschools be too great a strain on your family?

Each school has its own policies about twins and whether to keep them in the same classroom. Some schools let parents decide. Be sure the school policy is one you can live with and that you believe will be in the best interest of your children.

HOW DO PRESCHOOLS DECIDE WHO GETS IN?

Although every preschool strives for a balance of students, each program has its own method and priorities when it comes to selecting the incoming class. Virtually every school gives priority to siblings of current students, and some give preference to children in other categories, such as children of alumni or kids whose parents belong to the affiliated church or university. A few guarantee admission to children who belong in these groups, but most reserve the right to decline applicants if they find they're not a good fit or if the program can't meet their needs.

Most nursery schools want an even mix of boys and girls, with birthdays ranging throughout the year. Others seek to include a good mix of racial, ethnic, and socioeconomic backgrounds.

Real Parents Talk

We decided to rule out the programs that strongly encouraged or required twins to be separated. Knowing that our public elementary school would place them in different classes for kindergarten, we thought the adjustment of starting preschool was significant enough and didn't want to add to the anxiety by putting them in different classrooms. Once they had a good first school experience and got comfortable, they had no problems separating in elementary school.

—Ron S., Boston, Massachusetts

Personalities and temperaments may also be considered—no school wants a whole class full of either reserved or boisterous kids. And, of course, space is always a factor. If there are seventy-two families applying for only fifteen spaces, the school will have to make some tough decisions.

Remember, too, that selective preschools aren't looking only at your child. They're looking at the whole family. All schools want compatible families, with educational goals and values that are a good fit with the school. They're looking for parents who are supportive of their child's education and active in the school community. If you have useful or interesting skills that may benefit the school, that might work in your favor.

Criteria Preschools Consider

The preschool admissions process is an art, not a science. Every school has its own system of selecting applicants and weighs different factors in its own way. In addition to accommodating returning children, siblings, and others affiliated with the school, the director must try to balance the ages, sexes, personalities, and other factors that go into making up a class. Preschools look at some or all of the following things when deciding who gets in, not necessarily in this order:

- **Sex.** Most schools look for a fairly equal ratio of boys and girls.
- **Age.** Whether single-age or mixed-age classrooms, many preschools want to see birthdays scattered across the year.
- **Diversity.** Most schools try to create a diverse student body by accepting students from various races, ethnicities, socioeconomic backgrounds, neighborhoods, and family structures, as well as with a variety of temperaments.
- **Developmental readiness.** This is usually determined during the child interview, in parents' responses to application questions, and by recommendations from previous teachers. Schools look at social, language, and motor skills; attention span; ability to follow directions; and other criteria.
- **Affiliation with school.** Preference is usually given to siblings of current students because preschools know it's important to keep families together. Members of the church or synagogue a school is affiliated with, children of the school's alumni (legacies), children already enrolled in the toddler program, and children of school employees also usually

receive preferred admissions status.

- **What parents are like.** Schools want kids whose parents really want them to be there. They are looking for parents who understand the school's philosophy and are able to say why it would work well for their child.

They also want parents who are pleasant and who are excited to be involved in the preschool community. Schools can be turned off by parents who appear pushy or seem like they would be a nuisance to the school.

- **Knowing influential people.** It isn't necessary or expected that you'll know someone with pull, but it doesn't hurt to know a current or former parent, teacher, or member of the board who can make a phone call or write a letter of recommendation on behalf of your child.

Admissions Requirements

When applying to nursery schools, you'll be asked for some or all of the following:

- **Application fee.** Nursery schools charge anywhere from $10 to $100 or more just to apply, though a few don't charge at all. The application fee is generally nonrefundable, even if you're not offered admission or never get off the waiting list. Some schools will waive the fee for families with financial hardship.

- **Application form.** In addition to your contact information, you may be asked to respond to a few short-answer, or even essay, questions. Some schools may also request that additional materials be submitted along with the form, such as a recent photo, a health and immunization form, or a birth certificate.
- **School visit.** As discussed in the previous chapter, this might be an open house, a group tour, or an individual visit. Some schools require a tour before you can apply; others require an application before you can tour.
- **Child interview (regular admissions process).** This lets the school staff meet the child in person and assess his readiness for preschool. It might take the form of an observed playdate with other children or as an assessment where a teacher might test the child's developmental skills.
- **Parent interview (regular admissions process).** Meeting parents lets the staff get to know the families, and vice versa.
- **Student evaluation form or recommendation letter.** If your child is currently at another preschool, you might be asked for an evaluation of your child from his current teacher. Schools will usually also accept letters from others associated with the school, but it's not required or expected.

DOS AND DON'TS OF APPLYING

You can't control everything about the preschool application process, but there are plenty of steps you can take (and others you can avoid) to increase your odds of success.

Dos

- **Do read all applications and directions carefully.** Answer all questions completely and make sure nothing gets left out of the application packet before you turn it in.
- **Do keep organized.** Keep track of all the different schools' tour dates and application deadlines, and organize the applications, notes, and other paperwork by school.
- **Do be as flexible as you can about the schedule.** To increase your odds of getting into a competitive preschool, be open to afternoon sessions and different days of the week. This is particularly important if your child won't be entering at the youngest age allowed. Once your child enrolls, you can always ask to change the schedule later on.
- **Do let the school know how enthusiastic you are about the program and why.** Preschools want families who share their philosophy and are sincerely interested in their program. Try to mention to the director during the visit or in a thank-you letter why you love the school and why it's the right fit for your child. It won't guarantee you a spot, but it will increase your odds. If you have a top-choice school, let the director know—but only express this to one school (believe it or not, directors do talk to one another about applicants).
- **Do let the school know how you can be involved.** Do you have free time to volunteer at the school? Do you have a special skill or interesting job that could benefit the school, like party planning or web design?

Don'ts

- **Don't assume your child won't get in.** Never skip applying to a school just because you think it's too competitive, has a long waiting list, or you don't have an "in." Schools are looking for children and families they believe are a good fit and will contribute to the school community. Show this, and you'll have better odds than a family who has a connection and doesn't feel they need to put a lot of effort into the process.
- **Don't assume your child will get in.** Even if your cousin is on the board or your boss says she'll personally recommend your child to the director, never assume that's all it will take to get your child admitted. Take the admissions process seriously and demonstrate your interest in the program.
- **Don't try to bribe your way in.** Never give school officials the idea that you're trying to bribe them. Attending a fundraiser and bidding on a big ticket item is fine, but don't hint that you'll be very generous as a donor or that you can pay to renovate the building.
- **Don't stress out.** Last but not least, don't stress out too much. Remember, it's just preschool! If your child doesn't get into your first (or even third) choice of school, you'll still find someplace wonderful where he'll be happy and thrive.

If you live in New York City, which has its own unique way of doing things when it comes to admissions, be sure to read appendix 3 for more tips on applying. Otherwise, move on to chapter 9 to learn how to prepare a strong application.

Submitting a Strong Application

IT'S FINALLY TIME TO APPLY. First things first: you need an application. Some preschools let you download their application forms right off their website. Others only distribute applications at the school open house. With others, you'll need to call and have the school mail you an application, or drop by and pick it up from the school office.

All preschools will ask you for some basic information about your child and family (e.g., names, child's birth date), and some also ask several short, open-ended questions for you to answer in a few words or sentences. Although it's not as common, a few schools ask you to write a parent statement, which may consist of half- or full-page essays written in response to questions from the school or written freestyle by the parents.

GENERAL INFORMATION SECTION

This is the part of the application form that asks for all the basic information about your child and your family, including your names, your child's name and birth date, address, phone, email, any other preschools or day cares your child has attended, and your preferred schedule. Some may ask for details about your occupation or your child's general health. If the school is affiliated with a church or synagogue, it might ask if you're a member or for your religious background. Be sure all the answers you give are accurate and honest.

If you tend to be a neat freak, you might want to consider making copies of the application forms that aren't available online before you start filling them in. That way if you make a mistake (or your toddler spills juice on it), you'll have a clean copy to work with. You may want to start with the form that has the most fill-in-the-blank spaces so you can hunt down and collect all the information you'll need at once.

When the form is complete, double check everything to be sure that it's all correct and that all the spaces are filled in. Don't forget to sign and date the forms and include a check for the application fee, as well as any other required materials, such as a photo. It's a good idea to make a copy for your records before sending it in.

APPLICATION QUESTIONS

Short-answer and essay questions could be about anything from how you learned about the school to your child's favorite activities. These offer a chance to tell the preschool more about your child and your family, your reasons for applying to the school, and why you think your child will be a good match for the program. It's a golden opportunity to stand out and differentiate your child and your family from other applicants.

Responding to the questions will take some time and effort on your part, but be glad that you have a chance to personalize the application. Let the school know about your child's unique qualities and interests, about your family, and why you would complement the school community. If the school is down to a choice between your child and another child who's very similar, your responses may tip the balance in your favor.

Short-Answer Questions

If the school has asked for a short answer, get straight to the point and address the question directly. Don't make them read *War and Peace*. If the application asks for three adjectives describing your child, it's OK to write three words. If it asks for reasons you're considering the school, write a few sentences or simply list the characteristics of the program that appeal to you, depending on how much space is provided.

Parent Statements or Essays

Do some preschool applications really require essays—like college applications? Believe it or not, they do! This may seem like overkill, but try to see it as a positive. Generally, only schools with a very high number of applicants will ask for an essay. It helps the school screen out families who aren't seriously interested and won't make the effort to write a thoughtful essay and those who have educational goals different from the school's and may not be a good fit. So even though it can feel like a hassle (and a high school flashback), writing an essay will only benefit you. It will force you to think about what you're really looking for and what kind of environment will be best for your child.

Some nursery schools structure the parent statement by providing a few specific questions for you to respond to.

Others leave it slightly more open-ended and let you write what you want, though they might suggest the type of information they want you to share. It may be why you're applying to the program, your child's interests and activities, or her strengths and challenges.

> **Real Parents Talk**
>
> The application questions seemed simple enough, but because the school was extremely competitive, I couldn't help but overthink it and try to guess what kind of answer would impress them. Thankfully, my husband convinced me we should write from our gut. In the end, the most important thing was that the school impress us, not the other way around, and that we end up at a place that accepts us for who we are.
>
> —Sandra S., New York, New York

TIPS FOR WRITING

Some people are very comfortable just putting pen to paper and letting the words flow. Others are more hesitant or concerned that writing isn't their strength. Don't worry! These tips will help you write great short answers and essays.

1. **Start early.** Begin at least one or two weeks before the deadline, and plan to spend a few hours on each essay.

2. **Answer the question asked.** That seems simple, but read over what you've written to make sure you've answered the question and that the points you're trying to get across to the admissions committee about you and your child are clear. The rest is just filler that should be eliminated.

3. **Tailor your responses to each preschool.** The more personalized and less generic the answer, the more interested you seem and the better you show why the school is a good fit.

4. **Talk about why your family is a good match for the**

school. If the school prides itself on its active parent community, go ahead and talk about what types of events or committees you're interested in getting involved with.

5. **Show, don't just tell.** For essays, give specific examples or tell anecdotes about your child to illustrate major points. Your essay will be more memorable and the admissions committee will get a better picture of what you're saying.

6. **Write in your own words.** This isn't a master's thesis. Don't feel like you need to use big words or overly formal sentences. Preschools care more about what is written than how it's written.

7. **Proofread for spelling and grammar mistakes** before you submit everything.

COMMON APPLICATION QUESTIONS

The following are some of the most common short-answer and essay questions you might see on preschool applications. This section will help you understand why the question is being asked and give you tips for responding effectively and getting your point across in the best light possible.

1. How Did You Learn about Our School?

Nursery schools like to be able to track where applicants hear about them so they know which marketing efforts are most effective. They also want to know if you're connected to the school or know someone who is. Did a current parent refer you? Did you find the school during a web search? Did you or your spouse attend preschool there? Were you impressed at a preschool fair after talking with the director?

It doesn't really make a big difference how you found out

about the school. If you found the school on the Internet, great! The school will know its website is a good recruiting tool. However, if you do have a personal connection to the school, this is the time to mention it—even if it's just a parent you spoke with at the park.

2. Why Do You Wish to Send Your Child to Our School?

The application might also ask, "Why is our school a good fit for your child?" These types of questions are looking for you to show your understanding of how the program matches your child's and your family's needs. This is where you talk about the ways that this program in particular will be most appropriate for your child by addressing the goals from the previous question. For instance, describe how the school's educational philosophy matches your child's personality, interests, and your own parenting values. Or talk about how your creative child would love the weekly art class taught by a specialist, or how the play-based philosophy matches your desire for your child to develop her social skills. It will help you to go back and think about the criteria you used to choose the school in the first place.

It's important to tailor your response to the specific program, not just to preschool in general. Why did this school make your list? What is special about the curriculum, facilities, or teachers? Review the website and your notes from the visit and take note of what the preschool identifies as its own strengths, like its small class size, weekly field trips, or close-knit community. Mention specific things you saw, experienced, or heard during the school tour that particularly impressed you. If you spoke with someone who inspired you to apply, it doesn't hurt to mention his name and what great things he said about the program that made you want to apply.

Be sure you don't contradict the school's philosophy, and don't just talk about aspects that are purely logistical, like how the hours fit in with your work schedule. Tie the school's offerings to your child's needs to show you understand and value the program's specific features.

3. How Would You Describe Your Child?

The school might also ask, "Which adjectives best describe your child?" or "What are your child's interests, skills, and characteristics?" These questions are here for the school to get to know your child's personality and to give you a chance to distinguish her from all the other applicants. The admissions committee will also use this information to try to create a balanced class. For instance, if there are already a few active, energetic siblings coming into the class, they may be looking for some kids with a quieter and more reserved personality to add to the mix. The questions also help the committee ascertain your child's readiness for preschool (see chapter 13).

Brainstorm ways to describe your child and things she likes to do. If you're a little short of ideas, ask others (grandparents, baby-sitters, day-care providers) how they would describe her. Watch her while she plays. What kind of activities does your child enjoy (dancing to music, playing dress up, drawing)? What does she like to talk about? What is she good at?

Choose three to five things that your child is interested in and skills or personality traits to talk about (or adjectives, if that's what the question asks for). Try to pick traits that help show your child is ready for preschool, to be in a classroom environment, and to work cooperatively with others. If it's a short-answer question, you could demonstrate each one with a sentence or two. For example, "Zachary is very imaginative. He enjoys making up stories about animals at the zoo and acting them out." If it's an essay question, elaborate with anecdotes and stories to bring your child's personality to life. For instance, "Ava loves to cook. She puts on her apron and announces what she'll cook for the family in her toy kitchen. She carefully picks out a variety of plastic food, puts it in a bowl, stirs, and serves it to us. When we're done 'eating,' she always asks if it was yummy."

4. What Are Your Child's Greatest Strengths and Challenges or Weaknesses?

Asking about a child's strengths and weaknesses gives a good idea of how you see your child, how well you know her, and what things you know she can work on. It also gives the school a sense of what you as a parent consider strengths and challenges.

To most parents, this is kind of an odd question to ask about someone who's only two or three years old. It's similar to the previous question, in that the school uses it to learn about your child's personality and to help create a balanced class. Besides brainstorming on your own, ask others who know your child what they think her strengths and weaknesses are. Pay particular attention to physical, social, and emotional development. Choose two or three primary strengths and illustrate them with stories. Don't exaggerate her accomplishments or boast about how advanced your child is. Instead, focus on personality. Is she funny? Sensitive to others? Good at physical skills like climbing or stacking blocks? Think about the educational philosophy of the preschool—for a play-based preschool, for instance, don't mention only academic strengths.

For the weaknesses, one or two is plenty. Preschools know better than anyone that all children have something to work on, whether it's adapting to new places and people or having trouble sharing or cooperating with other children. Also, it's not a bad idea to note what you're doing at home to help your child learn more appropriate behavior.

5. Does Your Child Have Any Special Needs?

If your child has any special needs, the preschool needs to determine whether it can meet your child's specific requirements to ensure that she has a successful preschool experience.

You want the application to reflect the best about your child, so you may be tempted to skip this question. But if your child does have a disability or delay, she deserves to be in an environment that can support her. The school can't help your child if it doesn't know what she needs. If a preschool doesn't admit your child because it doesn't have the equipment or facilities she requires, or if it has a limit to the number of time-intensive children it can accommodate in the class, then that school isn't the right place for her anyway. It's better to be up front about what your child requires than to put her in a situation where she wouldn't feel safe or comfortable.

SAMPLE ESSAYS

Sometimes it's helpful to look at examples to get an idea of what you should be writing. Here's a preschool application essay written by a real parent. Of course, you don't want to just copy this. Your essay should be unique—after all, your child is.

SAMPLE ESSAY

What are you looking for in a preschool for your child?

We are looking for a preschool that will foster Nathan's independence, self-confidence, and curiosity, as well as help him learn how to treat others with kindness and respect. Since he is an only child, we believe he'll benefit greatly by making friends his own age and learning to share and cooperate with them.

We would like Nathan to get a head start on some basic academic skills, but we think preschool should primarily be a time for him to play, explore, and form friendships. Therefore, we would like him to be in a play-based classroom with teachers who support these endeavors, have extensive experience and training in early childhood development, and encourage him to grow at his own rate.

Preschool is going to be a big change for Nathan, as it will be his first time away from us. We want him to be in a program where he'll feel comfortable, be happy, and have fun. We know from our visit and talking to other parents that Bright Beginnings is the perfect school for him—a nurturing place that will make him feel secure and cared for while he's taking this important new step.

RECOMMENDATION LETTERS

Preschool Teacher or Day-Care Provider

If your child is attending another nursery school or day care, some schools will ask you to submit a letter of recommendation or a student evaluation form (which they provide) for the current teacher or day-care provider to fill out. It's important to ask the teacher as early as possible and give her whatever forms she'll need in plenty of time. Two to three weeks before the deadline is recommended.

Provide a stamped, self-addressed envelope and let the reference know what the deadline is. Make sure the reference has everything needed to write the letter, including the evaluation form from the prospective preschool and your contact information (you'll usually fill this in on the form itself). Give some insight into the preschool (a brochure and some of your own thoughts) so she'll know what kinds of things to talk about in the recommendation. After the teacher writes the letter, be sure to send her a thank-you note.

If you're leaving a preschool because you or your child isn't happy with it, be sensitive. If the teacher asks, let her know you're switching schools because the new one has characteristics not offered at the current school, such as a more convenient location or a smaller class size.

Individual Associated with the School

If a preschool you're interested in is very competitive, you might want to get an additional letter of recommendation if you know someone associated with the school, such as a parent, teacher, or board member who could share valuable information about your child. The person could also call or email the director on your child's behalf.

Don't assume that titles matter. It's better to have a parent or teacher at the school tell the director how great your kid is and how your family would be a great asset to the community than to have the chair of the school board send a generic letter that could apply to anybody. The reference should mention how he knows your family, why your child would be a good fit for the school, and some examples or anecdotes to show why. You may want to give your reference a copy of your application, especially if you wrote short answers or essays describing your child. Ask that your reference send the letter before the application deadline so the admissions committee can review it as part of your application package.

Don't worry if you don't have someone to do this for you. Most families don't submit an extra letter, including most of the ones who are accepted.

> ## Real Parents Talk
>
> She had been on the wait list at our favorite preschool for over a year, and I was anxious to get her enrolled before the birth of our second child. After making several follow-up calls with no results, I talked to a neighbor whose kid went to the school about my situation. She put in a good word for me, and she was accepted within days.
>
> —Mina P., Santa Monica, California

***

You've done all you can to make a good impression on paper. In the next chapter, you'll learn how to make a good impression in person. If none of the preschools you're applying to involve a child or parent interview, you can skip to chapter 11.

CHAPTER 10

Child and Parent Interviews

AFTER RECEIVING THE WRITTEN APPLICATIONS, some preschools will schedule an interview with the child, and sometimes with the parents as well. These usually take place a few weeks after you've turned in your paperwork. The child interview, which may involve playing with other children or working with a teacher one-on-one, is usually conducted separately from the parent interview (though they're often scheduled for the same day). Some schools, however, like to do a family interview with the parents and the child together.

As mentioned in chapter 7, preschools that don't conduct formal interviews may still be evaluating families during the school visits. So if you're asked to come in for a private tour with your child, the advice in this chapter will help prepare you in case you find yourself in an interview-like situation.

CHILD INTERVIEWS

The child interview lets the preschool staff meet and observe applicants in person. They'll be looking to see whether your child is developmentally ready for preschool and what his personality is like (Is he shy or extroverted? Calm or energetic?). When it comes to temperaments, there is no such thing as good or bad. Schools are looking to compose a class with a balance of personality types. When it comes to developmental readiness, every school is looking for similar skills, but each has its own priorities. For instance, a nursery school that uses a playdate-style interview likely focuses more on social interaction, whereas one that interviews kids individually is probably looking more at cognitive skills. In general, preschools consider the following:

- **How the child interacts with other children.** Does he share? Is he willing to take turns? Different children learn these skills at different ages, and the preschool will take that into account.
- **The child's ability to follow directions.** Your child doesn't have to do things perfectly, but he should be able to follow simple instructions, like how to sit in a circle or do an activity.
- **The child's ability to communicate clearly.** Can he ask for what he wants, or does he simply cry or point?
- **Attention span.** Can he sit still at circle time to hear a story? Does he finish an activity before moving on to another one or flit from one thing to another without finishing or putting materials away?
- **Fine and gross motor skills.** Fine motor skills include cutting with safety scissors or playing with play dough. Gross motor skills include activities like running, jumping, and performing songs with hand movements.
- **Ability to separate from parents.** Children aren't expected to separate from their parents as soon as they walk into an

unfamiliar classroom, but the teachers will take note if your child never leaves your side during the entire session.

Early childhood educators understand that not every child will have mastered every milestone by the age of two or three and that they can't get to know everything about a child in such a short time. But teachers and directors have a lot of experience—they know what to look for to determine whether the child will have a successful experience in a preschool setting. They don't want your child to be unhappy at preschool any more than you do. Most will try their best to make the interview fun for your child and not obvious that he's being observed or evaluated.

Child interviews can be held either one-on-one or in a group setting. Some schools want parents to be present during the interview; others want to observe the child without parents in the room. Find out ahead of time which method the preschool uses so you can let your child know what's going to happen at the preschool and what to expect.

Playdate

Schools often call the group interview a playdate, classroom visit, or child observation. The group interview is an opportunity for the staff to see how your child interacts with other children in a structured but relaxed social setting. Your child could spend anywhere from twenty minutes to two hours in a classroom with a group of other kids. The other children are usually other applicants, but they may be a mix of applicants and admitted siblings or children already enrolled from the year before.

The format usually follows part of a regular school day,

with circle time and free play, during which children can choose to play with puzzles, play dough, blocks, or other materials. The teacher might sing a song or read a story, and perhaps serve the kids a snack. Parents may be allowed to join circle time, or they may be asked to sit back while their child participates. Some schools ask parents to wait outside the room.

Assessment

Meeting with your child one-on-one lets a preschool gain insight into his developmental readiness and get to know his personality better. The teacher or director might do some activities with him, like coloring, puzzles, or reading a book. Nursery schools call this an assessment, screening, or testing. In addition to testing your child's general knowledge and physical skills, assessments help schools gauge a child's ability to communicate verbally, to focus on a task, and to follow directions. They may look for how well your child can

- identify numbers, letters, colors, and shapes
- sort objects by size or color

- run, jump, or walk in a line
- draw, build blocks, or cut with safety scissors
- respond to questions along the lines of age, full name, and what he likes to play.

Again, preschools know to expect that abilities vary among two-, three- and four-year-olds.

Your Role in the Child Interview

Little about the admissions process causes parents as much anxiety as the child interview. Will your outgoing, cooperative child suddenly become clingy and whiny? Will he have a temper tantrum or snatch a toy from another kid's hand? Don't worry. The teachers have been there before. They don't expect young kids to walk into the classroom with all their social and academic skills already in place. Teachers deal with different personalities every day and understand that some children are shy and take time to warm up in a new environment. Preschools like to have a variety of temperaments in the classroom. Don't assume your child's personality on that day will automatically exclude him.

That said, let the preschool conduct the interview in its own way, and let your child be himself. Before you leave the house, show him with your own behavior that you think this visit will be fun. If parents can't sit in on the interview, let your child know that you'll be right outside, waiting for him when he's done.

There's not much you can do to change your child's mood during the visit. Especially if your child is being cranky or timid, your being calm and encouraging will have a much better effect than will pushing him to participate if he's reluctant. If a teacher is trying to talk to your child or engage him in an activity, don't interrupt or answer questions for him. Remember, even during your child's interview, the staff may be evaluating you as well. It makes a better impression if you stay relaxed and act supportive.

Even if you're nervous, don't forget to use this time to make your own observations about the school and the staff. Like a job interview, they're evaluating you, but you should be evaluating them at the same time. Don't miss this prime opportunity to see how teachers and administrators work with parents and children. Was the staff warm and friendly? Did the teachers make you and your child feel at ease? These are important observations that you'll need during your decision-making process.

TIPS FOR THE CHILD INTERVIEW

- Avoid scheduling the interview during your child's nap time or when he might be tired and cranky. Also, make sure he has eaten beforehand.
- Tell your child what to expect, including whether you'll be in the same room during the interview.
- Be careful about bribing your child to behave well—he might tattle on you to the teacher. An ice-cream cone is probably OK; a new tricycle isn't.
- Dress your child casually, comfortably, and neatly—the sort of clothes he'll be wearing to preschool.
- Bring the school's address and directions with you when

you leave the house. Give yourself time to find a place to park.

· Arrive a few minutes early. If you have to be late or cancel, call the school right away to let someone know or to reschedule.

· If your child wasn't acting like himself, and later you find he had a 102-degree fever, let the school know. You may be able to set up another visit.

Should I Coach My Child?

You might feel tempted to try to coach your child in the days or weeks leading up to the interview. Resist this temptation. First of all, kids this age can't be coached to do "better" at this kind of experience. More important, you don't want your child to feel nervous, pressured, or afraid of letting you down, which can lead to problems at the interview—the opposite of what you were coaching him for!

The best preparation you can give your child—whether for the child interview or for preschool as a whole—is to engage him in learning in his everyday life. Get him in the habit of taking turns on the slide at the playground or of counting how many carrots are left on his plate. Toddlers are naturally curious about the world and absorb information like sponges, especially if it's done in a fun way. For more ideas on preparing your child for preschool, see chapter 13.

PARENT INTERVIEWS

Some nursery schools want to meet parents before they admit a child. These interviews usually happen individually, but sometimes they take place in a group with other parents.

This is a way for the school to get to know you better and find out your perspective on your child, and for you to learn about the program and ask questions. For many, the parent interview is even more nerve-racking than the child interview! Not to worry—most schools try to make it a relaxed, two-way conversation. Even if you do find yourself in a more formal question-and-answer situation, think of it as an opportunity for you to meet school staff, to get a sense of the school culture, and to find out whether the program is right for your family.

The parent interview usually happens during or right after the child interview. Some schools take advantage of the child's playdate to talk to parents, either in the same room or in another room. It's important for both parents to attend and participate in the conversation. (This goes for separated and divorced parents, too, if they both live in the area.) You'll want to show that both of you are committed to supporting your child's education and to learning about the program.

The interviewer may be the director, a teacher, or a school administrator on the admissions committee. Some schools focus more on learning about the child. Others want to get to know the parents better. Questions you might be asked include the following:

- Why are you interested in our school?
- How does your child like his current preschool or day-care experience?
- Tell me about your child. What is he interested in?
- What are your educational goals for your child? What would you like him to get out of his preschool experience?

- How often does he socialize with other children? How does he get along with others?
- How do you handle discipline at home?
- What else would you like to know about the school?

> **Real Parents Talk**
>
> Our meeting with the director was very relaxing. I didn't feel judged in any way. It really felt more like a chance for us to learn more about the school and ask questions of them.
>
> —Leonard W., Atlanta, Georgia

TIPS FOR THE PARENT INTERVIEW

- Both parents should attend the interview, if possible.
- Leave room in your schedule for the interview to run late so you won't be checking your watch. Turn off your cell phone before you arrive.
- Schedule interviews at your favorite school last so you can learn from previous experience.
- Review the website and marketing materials before the interview so you can prepare questions that aren't already in the school's available literature. Reread your notes from the school visit and your application essays.
- Talk to your spouse or partner about the interview the night before. Be sure you're on the same page in terms of what you like about the school, your child's strengths, and so on.

Surviving the Parent Interview

It's important to be honest and to be yourself. Of course, you want to let the interviewer know that you are seriously interested in their program and that your family would be a great addition to the community. But resist the urge to act like a different person or give "better" answers that you think they want to hear. Be friendly, respectful, and make eye contact.

Schools want to hear about your child's strengths as well as areas where he's still developing. They want to know your goals for your child as a preschool student. Give them some examples that show his personality, his readiness for preschool, and the ways that you spend time together. Stories and anecdotes help you make a memorable impression. Go ahead and tell the story of the time he wore his Halloween costume every day for a month.

Describe your child as he is—not as a list of accomplishments or as some unbelievably perfect angel. Schools are looking for a variety of personalities, so don't be afraid to tell them that your child is quiet, talkative, outgoing, or hasn't had a lot of experience socializing with others. Be forthcoming about any developmental issues he's struggling with (especially if they might show up in a playdate) and about what you're doing to help. It's OK to say he has occasional temper tantrums—use that opportunity to explain how you handle them. Let the preschool staff be confident that you are parents who care about your child and are able and willing to work with them as a team to support him.

Talk about why the program interests you and why you're enthusiastic about its educational approach. Think about why you chose the school in the first place and how you think your child will benefit from the program. You don't have to be an expert in early childhood education to talk about why a particular school appeals to you. Describe some of the things you saw on the tour or heard about from other parents that piqued your interest. The staff is proud of their program—show that you understand why.

Don't Forget to Ask Questions

Don't forget that you're also interviewing the school. Have some questions ready to ask (you can find examples in chapter 7). Schools appreciate parents who are curious about the program and want to learn more. They'll be happy to tell you about their teachers' experience, educational philosophy, curriculum, or ways parents can get involved. The kinds of questions you ask will help the staff understand you and your values, and they'll show that you've put some thought into choosing a preschool.

Congratulations—the application process is finally over! In the next chapter, we'll talk about the kinds of responses you might get and how to choose the nursery school you'll ultimately send your child to. In the meantime, try to relax and find something else to think about while you're waiting to hear back from all the preschools.

CHAPTER 11

Making the Final Decision

THE TIME HAS COME TO decide where to enroll your child. Take a moment to appreciate being at the end of this long process—you don't have to start worrying about kindergarten for at least another year!

Starting preschool is a big milestone in your child's young life, and you want to make the right choice. It's important to remember a few things:

- There is no one "perfect" preschool.
- There are many nursery schools that will work for your child's needs and personality and provide a wonderful learning experience that will prepare her for kindergarten.
- A preschool's reputation or popularity is less important than whether you feel comfortable with the teachers and the school's educational approach.

If you find yourself wavering between preschools, go back to your original selection criteria. Review your side-by-side comparison of the programs to see which more closely matches your preferences for location, schedule, teacher-student ratio, and other factors. You can ask the schools for a second visit with your child to look more closely at each one and to see how your child reacts to the environment. (Remember, once you receive the notification you won't have a lot of time to make a decision, so if you want a second visit, you'll need to move quickly to set it up.) Talk to parents you know who have kids in the school, or ask for names of current parents you can call. You might hear something that helps you make a choice.

You also need to take your own needs into account, as well as your child's. Maybe the neighborhood school is more convenient, but it's worth driving a little farther to send your child to a language-immersion program. Or you may choose a preschool with a slightly higher teacher-student ratio but a lower tuition and teachers who are just as great. If considering all the information you've gathered one more time doesn't bring you to a firm decision, go with your gut. If the school feels right, then it is right.

No matter which school you choose, be sure your child can see that you're happy and excited about the new adventure your family is taking. Your child will be taking her cues from you, especially at first, about whether she should be looking forward to preschool.

At the end of the day, remember that it probably won't make that much of a difference if you send your child to your first-choice school or to any one of the schools you chose to apply to. You've done the work to know that they're all good programs and that your child would be successful in any of them. And remember, it's just preschool. This decision will affect your child's life for the next few years. But no matter what anyone tells you, she'll still have a chance of getting into an Ivy League university (if that's your goal) regardless of which preschool she attends!

BUT WE STILL HAVEN'T HEARD

If you hear from your second-choice preschool before you've heard from your top choice, you may be in the difficult position of needing to send in a deposit to secure a spot. If this happens to you, call the school that accepted your child and ask whether the deadline can be extended. Then, call your first-choice school, explain the situation, and ask whether it's possible for the school to expedite the decision. Schools are inundated with frantic calls from parents the week after letters go out, so be persistent and make an effort to actually speak with a school administrator rather than just leaving a voice-mail message.

The truth is that you may not be able to reach someone, or the schools might not be able to make an exception for you. In that case, you may have to send in the tuition deposit for the school you've heard from to secure the spot and forfeit the money if your first-choice school later accepts your child. Otherwise, if you don't get good news from your first-choice school, your child could be left without any preschool to attend.

WE'VE BEEN WAIT-LISTED—WHAT NOW?

If your child was put on the waiting list at a preschool, that means that the school doesn't have a space for her right now, but she may be admitted if one opens up. This will occur if another admitted family chooses not to enroll or if a current family decides to leave the program.

If a school with a rounds admission policy wait-listed your child, keep in mind that this type of waiting list is usually more of a waiting pool and not strictly prioritized (you don't have a number). These schools know that a certain percentage of families receiving acceptance letters will choose other programs and that the children who do enroll in the first round may not fill up a class, so the school places additional applicants on the waiting list. When someone declines an acceptance offer, the school will offer that spot to a child on the waiting list (probably with a similar profile), so there's some luck involved.

When you receive notice that your child is on a waiting list, you'll need to decide whether you want her to remain there. There's no guarantee that your child will ultimately be admitted before the school year begins, and even if she is, you may not hear until after decision deadlines at other schools have passed. If your child is wait-listed at your top-choice school, you can go ahead and commit to your favorite school that offered admission (unless you live in New York City*). It will mean, however, sending in your deposit and forfeiting the money if your top-choice school comes through. These waiting lists are usually not continued from year to year, so if you want to try again for the next year, you'll have to repeat the application process.

Although this system works well for the schools, it can be very hard on parents. There are some things you can try,

---

*According to guidelines set by the Independent Schools Admission Association of Greater New York, once parents sign an enrollment contract with an ISAAGNY school, no other ISAAGNY school can offer the child a spot. Check the website at www.isaagny.org for details and a list of member schools.

however, to improve your chances of getting the next available spot:

- **Call the director.** Within a day or two after receiving your admissions letter, pick up the phone. Be courteous and let the director know that you're pleased your child is still being considered and that you're definitely interested in enrolling her. Mention what impresses you about the school and why you think it's a great fit for your child. If you're absolutely certain that you would enroll if accepted, tell the director so. Ask how likely it is that a space will open up; how often you should follow up; and whether the director prefers phone calls, email, or mailed notes.
- **Write a compelling letter to the director (nicely) expressing your disappointment, and reiterate some of the things you mentioned on the phone.** Explain why you love the program and why it's a great fit for your child. Let the director know that you hope your child will be admitted if a space opens up. It doesn't hurt to mention how you would contribute (not financially!) to the school community.
- **Ask for a phone call or letter of support from someone you know, such as a parent, administrator, board member, or someone else closely associated with the school.** If this person already submitted a letter of recommendation, a phone call or email would be more appropriate.
- **Follow up to show your continued interest, but don't go overboard.** Keep in touch—but not more often than the school says to. Calling or sending a note at least once in the middle of the summer and once at the end of the summer is appropriate, unless the director says otherwise.

- **Enroll your child in the summer program if the preschool offers one.** Sending your child to the summer camp lets the staff get to know her and clearly reinforces your commitment to the school.
- **Visit the school again to show your interest.** Perhaps attend a school event or a fundraiser that's open to the public. Reintroduce yourself to the director, but don't expect him to have a lengthy conversation with you.
- **Be persistent, not a pest.** You don't want to be known as that annoying parent who wouldn't stop calling or who was rude and disrespectful to the staff. Don't give the director updates on your child's latest accomplishments ("He can count to twenty!" "She's taking Mandarin!"). Being a nuisance doesn't do anything to help your child's chances of getting into the school. So be pleasant, show interest, and leave a good impression.
- **Don't get discouraged.** There is a chance your child will still get in this year. Spaces free up as families move or accept other preschool offers. Be patient and stay in touch with the director. When a spot opens up, the preschool will know that it only has to make one call to fill it. And if your child doesn't end up getting a spot, your persistence and enthusiasm for the school will give you a leg up if you decide to reapply the following year.

OUR FAVORITE PRESCHOOL TURNED US DOWN— WHAT NOW?

The unthinkable has happened. Your child did not get accepted to your top-choice preschool.

First of all, it happens. It's hard not to take a preschool

rejection personally. You may well feel disappointed, upset, and even angry. But remember—preschools reject applicants for any number of reasons. Even if the director loved your child and your family and really wanted you to join the school, he might have had to give most of the spaces to siblings. Or the school may use a first-come, first-served admissions policy and the class filled up before the school got to your child's place on the list.

If you choose, you could call the director and ask for any feedback about your application. Was there anything you could have done differently to change the outcome? Especially if there was a child assessment, the director may be open to telling you if he felt your child wasn't developmentally ready for preschool. But in most cases, schools won't have any specific feedback to offer. They will probably explain that it's a difficult, complicated process; that there were many applicants; and that they chose children who would round out the class of siblings who had already been accepted.

No matter what someone tells you, be very polite—never demanding—to whomever you talk with from the school. That person is doing you a favor by answering your questions, so be respectful. You'll want to keep a favorable impression, especially if you're interested in reapplying next year.

Wherever your child ultimately goes to preschool, she'll have a wonderful experience. You didn't apply to any schools you weren't comfortable with, remember? So if she goes to number two, three, or four on your list, she'll still be able to learn everything she needs to know to be ready for kindergarten, and she'll have a great time doing it.

OUR CHILD DIDN'T GET A SPOT AT ANY PRESCHOOL— WHAT ARE OUR OPTIONS?

It's not likely but it is possible that your child doesn't receive an acceptance at any preschool. Even if this happens, try not to panic. It's not the end of the world. But you do need to carefully consider your options. The first thing to do is cope with your emotional reaction. Chances are that you never imagined you'd be in this situation. Remind yourself that there are many factors in the preschool admissions process that are beyond your control. You may have applied to schools with extremely long waiting lists, to very few schools, or to small or highly competitive programs.

Try not to feel as if your family has been judged negatively or been slighted by the preschool. The decisions are not a judgment from the school (or society as a whole) on your child or on your parenting skills. Don't think of a preschool rejection as a personal failure. And especially don't think of it as your child's failure. Don't give her any indication that you're disappointed. Remember to stay calm and consider your other options.

Yes, you do have other options. If your child was placed on the waiting list at any school, follow the tips in the previous section to maximize your chances of her being accepted. Also, consider the following options:

- **Try to find other preschools that have spaces still available.** Contact schools you considered but didn't apply to, and ask friends and neighbors (maybe even the director of one of the schools that didn't accept your child, if you have a good rapport) if they know of any programs with spaces. Preschools that are fairly new or in a neighborhood with less demand may still have open spots.

- **Apply to other preschools that have rolling admissions.** Even if your child doesn't start in September, she could still be placed in preschool during this school year.

- **Opt out of preschool for this year, and reapply next year.** Depending on your child's age, you may want to skip a year of preschool, or skip preschool altogether. After all, it's not man-

> ### Real Parents Talk
>
> We didn't get into any of the pre-schools we applied to, so I signed her up for a three-hour Mandarin class for preschool-aged kids a few days a week. They have circle time, arts and crafts, and do the same activities as any other preschool—and she gets to do it all while learning a foreign language.
>
> —Cathy H., San Diego, California

datory, and people who never went to preschool still go on to live full lives! Instead, sign your child up for drop-off classes. Try art, music, or gym classes, where she'll get an opportunity to socialize with other kids and experience a classroom setting without you in the room. You could even coordinate with a few other families to create an informal co-op preschool playgroup, with or without a professional teacher. (Think of the tuition dollars you'll save!)

ACCEPTING AN OFFER

In all the excitement of receiving acceptance letters, making phone calls, and getting advice from others, don't forget to accept your spot and send in your deposit before the deadline! You should also contact all the other nursery schools as soon as possible to let them know that you've chosen another school. You can call (a voice-mail message is fine) or send a short thank-you note declining the invitation to attend. This is important because there's another child out there on a waiting list whose parents are hoping for that spot.

Also, be sure to call anyone who wrote a recommendation on your family's behalf to the preschool that you've chosen to give them the good news. They may have some great advice on what to expect from the program.

Before you know it, the frantic preschool admissions process is over. You and your child are on your way to a new chapter in your lives—starting preschool! In the next chapter, you'll learn some tips to help pay for your child's nursery school education.

CHAPTER 12

Paying for Preschool

IT OFTEN COMES AS QUITE a shock to many new parents, but preschool can be expensive. In fact, some parents end up spending more on their child's nursery school each year than they did for their own college tuition. But don't worry—if you're willing to put in a little effort, there are things you can do to make preschool more affordable.

Think about how much you can afford to pay, and evaluate the schools with your budget in mind. Cost shouldn't be your only criteria, or the most important one, but you'll find that in most cases a moderately priced nursery school will provide all the same benefits to your child—or at least the ones that matter most—that a more expensive one will. Sure, maybe you'd love to send your child to the preschool with the newest facility, a huge outdoor play area, organic hot lunches, and a working farm. But if the preschool down the block has a great educational program and a warm, welcoming staff for a lower price, thinking about your budget can help you make the wiser choice for your family.

DETERMINE YOUR BUDGET

Although preschool may not be cheap, it's a worthwhile expense, and it has both immediate and lasting benefits. But preschool tuition doesn't have to break the bank. With a little planning and a few strategies in place, you can keep the costs within your budget.

What Are You Already Paying For?

To figure out what you can afford to pay, start by determining what you already pay for child care during the day. Add up the costs of your child's activities, classes, outings, babysitting or a nanny during school hours, educational supplies and toys for home, and meals at home that the preschool will now provide. Then you can plan to redirect that money toward school tuition.

Where Can You Cut Existing Costs?

Factoring in your existing costs will put you on your way toward covering the costs of preschool. But if you need more money to cover tuition and other expenses, think about your current spending habits and figure out what you might be able to do without for a few years. Sometimes very small changes that save only a little bit of money at a time really add up over the course of a year. Try packing your own lunch instead of eating out and cutting back on buying takeout for dinner—you can save more than a thousand dollars a year. If you spend $2 on coffee every morning at a coffee shop, make your own coffee at home or work, and you can save $500 annually. If you have a housekeeper come every week, could you live with cleaning once a month instead or cutting that service out altogether? Think of other ways you can be more economical—can you do without buying new clothes, your health club membership, magazine subscriptions, or cable television (or at least the premium channels)?

Look at your monthly expenses to see where you can cut costs. Then add the savings you find to the amount you can spend for preschool (as calculated previously). The total is the amount you can afford for nursery school expenditures. A few dollars here and there can make a big difference in the long run.

KEEPING PRESCHOOL COSTS DOWN

There are several things you can do to keep the costs of preschool down. By following any of the strategies here, you can cut your annual costs by a significant amount:

- **Look into part-time and co-op programs.** The less time your child spends in school, the less you'll be paying. If you don't mind putting in some time and effort to help run the school, consider enrolling in a co-op program to reduce costs even further. If you need child care on days your child is not in school, share a baby-sitter with another family or offer to switch off with another preschool parent so that each of you watches both kids on alternating days.
- **If you need full-time care, consider a child care center with a preschool program.** Sometimes parents overlook the day-care option, but many centers are high-quality preschools, and the cost per hour for such schools may be less once you factor in the cost of extended care at other nursery schools. Don't forget the cost of (and time to find) child care on

all the days that school is closed or closes early, such as parent-teacher conferences and vacation weeks—child care centers generally don't close for these nearly as often as regular preschools do.

- **Wait a year or two.** Just because the preschool you like starts at two years old doesn't mean your child has to start then. Starting at three or even four years old is acceptable, if not more common. Or start him part time at an earlier age to secure a spot now, and then ramp up to a full-time schedule the following year. In the meantime, teach your child what he'd be learning in nursery school yourself. Sign up for classes so he is exposed to being in a classroom setting, go on field trips, and set up regular playdates with other kids so your child has a chance to learn socialization skills.

- **Look into public pre-K programs.** Public pre-K programs may be low cost or even free, depending on where you live. Eligibility differs by city and state, and in most states, low-income families and children with special needs get preference. See chapter 1 for more information. If you're interested in a program like this, call your local school district to find out more.

- **Don't go overboard buying back-to-school clothes or other unnecessary items.** Just because your child will be in preschool doesn't mean he needs an entirely new wardrobe. He definitely doesn't need a whole new one by the first day.

- **Look for a sibling discount.** If at some point you'll have more than one child enrolled at the same time, look for a school that offers a tuition discount for younger siblings (usually between 5 percent and 20 percent). That could add up to several hundreds, if not thousands, of dollars in savings.

Every school has parents who are working hard to afford private preschool, so don't feel like you're the only one who has to make some changes and stretch a bit to afford this new expense. There are plenty of people in the same boat.

FINANCIAL AID

In addition to cutting your own expenses and reallocating money in your own budget, your preschool may be able to help with the costs as well. Many preschools offer financial aid on the basis of a family's need. If you need financial assistance, be sure to apply for it at the same time that you apply for admission. The deadlines may not be exactly the same, so check with each school, and make sure to stay on top of everything you need to do and when you need to do it. Many schools hold financial aid workshops to explain the types of aid available and the procedures and time lines for applying. Most likely, you'll need to fill out some forms and provide documents such as your W-2 and tax return that help schools figure out how much you can afford to contribute toward school expenses. After subtracting this amount from their tuition and fees, schools look at the remaining amount needed and weigh it against their financial aid funds to figure out how much money they can give.

Each school has its own financial aid policy, which could include the following:

- **Sliding-scale tuition.** This program offers reduced tuition according to family income. Private and public preschools that charge tuition make use of this type of program.
- **Loans.** Offered either directly from the school or through

an outside agency, loans enable you to borrow money to help pay for tuition. But loans mean debt, so think carefully before accepting loans for preschool.

- **Payment plans.** This type of program, which is quite common, lets you pay in interest-free, monthly installments so that you don't have to pay the entire year's tuition bill up front when school starts. There might be a small fee to sign up for such programs, however.

- **Scholarships.** Although scholarships are not very common for preschool education, some schools or outside community or religious organizations award scholarship money to low-income families.

If you're seriously considering a preschool but don't think you can afford the tuition, it's worth the effort to apply for financial aid—even if you think your income is too high to qualify. At some schools, families making more than $150,000 a year may still be eligible for a break on tuition, so don't make any assumptions. Besides your income, schools also consider your assets (such as your savings and your home's value), how many children in your family are attending

> ### Real Parents Talk
>
> We were excited to get accepted to our first-choice school but knew we could not afford to send her because initially we did not get any financial aid. After calling the financial aid director and telling her of our concerns, she asked if there were any special financial commitments for our family that the school should know about that might help qualify us for sliding-scale tuition. There were, so they were able to give us a 20 percent break in tuition, which allowed us to enroll her.
>
> —Eric Y., San Francisco, California

tuition-paying schools, and any unusual expenses (such as high medical costs).

Don't worry that applying for assistance will hurt your child's chances of admission. Although your child's admission doesn't guarantee that you'll receive any financial aid (or as much as you'd like), preschools generally don't reject qualified applicants because of their financial need. In fact, many programs strive for a socioeconomically diverse student body and take pride in being able to provide financial support to families that need it.

DEPENDENT-CARE FLEXIBLE SPENDING ACCOUNT

Many employers offer a flexible spending account (FSA) for dependent care that lets you set aside up to $5,000 before taxes to pay for work-related child care expenses, including a licensed preschool or day care, after- or before-school care, day camp, or a baby-sitter or nanny. Both parents (if married) need to be working to qualify for such an account, so unfortunately, if one parent works but the other stays at home, even the working spouse can't participate in this type of plan. The only exception is if the stay-at-home parent is a full-time student or disabled—in that case, you're allowed to participate in the FSA, but the IRS deems that spouse's income during the time he or she is a student to be $250 per month for one child or $500 per month for more than one child. Your FSA contribution can't exceed the annual income of the spouse who earns less, so if you make $60,000 and your spouse makes $2,500, you can only set aside a maximum of $2,500.

By contributing to a dependent-care account directly from your paycheck and paying for some or all of your nursery school tuition with pretax dollars, you'll lower your taxable income and thereby save money. In 2010, the maximum allowed family contribution to an FSA was $5,000 for the year for single parents and couples filing jointly ($2,500 each for married individuals filing separate returns). Employers may choose to set a limit lower than $5,000, however. Your marginal tax rate determines your tax savings—the higher your tax rate, the greater are your tax savings.

The Dependent Care Account comparison chart that follows shows an example of how this type of account can save you money: Let's say that you earned $50,000 and paid $4,500 in eligible child care or preschool expenses for one child. In this scenario, you would have saved $1,350 a year just by contributing to a dependent-care account. Keep in mind that this example is for illustration purposes only; your actual tax savings will depend on several factors, including your income, standard and other tax deductions, your tax bracket, and dependent-care costs, among other things.

Dependent-Care Account Example

	With Dependent Care Reimbursement	Without Dependent Care Reimbursement
Annual Salary	$50,000	$50,000
Less Dependent Care Contribution	($4,500)	
Taxable Income	$45,500	$50,000
Less Federal & Social Security Taxes	($12,150)	($13,500)
Less Preschool Expense (Out-of-Pocket)	$0	($4,500)
Take Home Pay	$33,350	$32,000
Savings	$1,350	$0

To sign up for an FSA, once a year your employer will ask how much you want to contribute. With each paycheck, your employer will deduct a proportionate amount of that total. To get reimbursed from your account, all you need to do is submit a form and the receipts for the expenses to the plan administrator, who will reimburse you the money. Certain rules apply regarding how and when the money is disbursed, so be sure to read all the fine print and keep any tuition and other child care–related receipts.

Also, make sure you plan carefully and contribute only as much as you'll need for preschool and other eligible child care, as the IRS has a use-it-or-lose-it rule that requires you to forfeit any money you don't use by the end of the year. Unless you have a qualified life event, such as a new baby or your spouse changes jobs, you won't be able to stop your contributions or change the amount in the middle of the year.

CHILD CARE TAX CREDIT

The federal government offers a tax break in the form of the Child and Dependent Care Tax Credit to help families pay for child care while parents are working. A tax credit is much better than a deduction, which just lowers the income you use to calculate your taxes. Essentially, a credit is like free money from the IRS—the dollars are subtracted right from your tax bill, so if you owe $1,000 in taxes and get a $600 credit, you'll end up only paying $400. This tax credit isn't refundable, however, so if your credit is more than the amount of taxes you owe, you won't get a refund.

The credit ranges from 20–35 percent of the first $3,000 of your child care costs for one child. The percentage is based on your income, so the more you earn, the lower the amount of your tax credit. For instance, if your income was $43,000 or more in 2010, you would have been entitled to a 20 percent credit. That's a kickback of $600 (20 percent x $3,000) if you paid $3,000 or more for the care of one child. You qualify for the maximum credit of 35 percent only if you have very low income (less than $15,000 in 2010). As with an FSA, to be eligible for the tax credit, both spouses (if married) must be working (with the exception of a spouse who is a full-time student or disabled—see the previous section for more information), and the child care expenses to which you apply the credit can't exceed the income of the spouse who earns less.

You can claim both the child care credit and your employer's dependent-care FSA, but you can't double dip and use expenses that could be reimbursed through an FSA to also claim the tax credit. This means that you will not be able to claim the child care credit for one kid if you had more than $3,000 in contributions to your FSA. So for instance, if your preschool tuition is $7,000 and your employer's FSA allows you to contribute a maximum of $2,500, you would subtract $2,500 from $3,000 (the expense limit for one child for the child care credit). As a result, you can only claim $500 worth of expenses for the credit. Say your child care tax credit is 20 percent of the $500, or $100. If the same scenario applied but you contributed $5,000 to your FSA, you would not be able to claim the tax credit at all. (But if you had two children in child care and contributed $5,000 to an FSA, you would be able to claim $1,000 in expenses for the child care credit, because the expense limit for two kids is $6,000). Most families, particularly those with only one child, get a bigger tax break with an FSA than with claiming the credit. To determine which is better for you, talk to a tax adviser.

To learn more about the Child and Dependent Care Tax Credit and determine what you're eligible to receive, visit the IRS's website at www.irs.gov and download Publication 503, "Child and Dependent Care Expenses," or call the IRS toll-free at 1-800-829-1040.

State Child Care Tax Credit

In addition to the federal tax credit, some states have their own dependent-care tax credits. Unlike the federal program, some state tax credits are even refundable, which means you can get a tax refund if the credit is more than the amount of taxes you owe. If your state has this type of credit, you can file a claim both in your state taxes and in your federal taxes. To learn more, contact your state tax or revenue office or your local Child Care Resource and Referral (CCR&R) agency. You can find your local CCR&R at www.childcareaware.org or by calling 1-800-424-2246.

CHILD CARE SUBSIDIES

Child care subsidy programs are available in all states for working families that earn low incomes, primarily through a federal program called the Child Care and Development Fund. Each state has its own eligibility requirements. For instance, some states provide subsidies to working families that earn less than double the federal poverty level (the equivalent of $36,620 for a family of three in 2010). Subsidy amounts are calculated on a sliding scale based on income, so families making more would receive a smaller subsidy than those with lower incomes.

Besides income, other criteria can apply as well: parents may have to be working or looking for work, in school, or homeless.

The subsidy can come in the form of vouchers to parents or payments made directly to the participating provider, which is usually a preschool or day care (though some states include baby-sitters as well). To find out about child care subsidy programs in your area, contact your state's Department of Social Services or your local CCR&R (www.childcareaware. org)—and do so as early as possible, as some states have waiting lists for families.

CHAPTER 13

Preschool Readiness Skills

IT'S EXCITING TO LOOK FORWARD to a new experience like preschool, especially once you know where your child will be attending. Long before her first day of school, however, you can help your child build the skills she'll need to have a successful preschool experience.

Although your child's preschool teacher will be a significant force in your child's development once school begins, you are your child's most influential teacher. By incorporating learning activities in everyday life—reading, talking, playing with others, exploring the playground—you can give her the skills she needs to be comfortable and happy in a preschool setting. The important thing at this age is for learning to be fun. Preschool-age kids shouldn't feel like learning is a chore.

This chapter will go over the social, physical, and cognitive skills that will help her get ready to be in a classroom environment. Don't worry if she doesn't do all or even most of the skills listed here. If your child is just given the chance to practice them, she'll have an easier time adjusting to preschool.

Every child develops at her own rate, and a four-year-old will have very different skills than a two- or three-year-old. In addition, the preschool's expectations of its students will vary depending on the teacher and the curriculum. If you do have any questions or concerns regarding your child's development, you should talk to your pediatrician.

SOCIAL AND EMOTIONAL SKILLS

Preschool is the time when children begin to learn social and emotional skills that they'll use throughout their lives. In preschool, children need to be able to get along with others when playing and learning together. They need to be able to sit relatively still and listen during group activities like circle time and story time. These things may seem simple, but they are very important for proper social development and affect how they interact with the outside world. Give your child opportunities to begin developing these skills even before preschool begins.

Getting Along with Others

One of the most important benefits of preschool for children is learning to socialize in a group setting and get along with others by sharing, taking turns, being respectful of others, and playing cooperatively. It helps if kids have practice resolving conflicts on their own and learning to use their words to communicate rather than hitting or yelling. By understanding how to behave and interact appropriately around their classmates, they'll find it easier to make friends, avoid scuffles, and have fun in preschool ahead of her.

Give your child lots of opportunities to socialize with others her age and practice these skills. Visit the playground, arrange playdates with one or two other kids, or enroll in a toddler music or gym class. Be supportive and encourage her to work out problems in a positive way. For example, if your child and her friend are arguing over a toy, instead of just telling her to share, show her that there are different ways to solve the problem ("While you're waiting for Sophie to finish playing with the oven, would you like to sit with me and read a book or play with the doll house?"). Let your child know when she's done a good job. If you see her sharing with a friend, say something like, "That was very nice of you to share your crayons with Madison. Your friends at preschool are going to be happy when you share with them."

Expressing Needs, Wants, and Feelings

By preschool age, kids should be able to use simple sentences to say what they want and how they're feeling. A three-year-old might say, "I'm thirsty" or "I have to go potty," whereas four-year-olds should be able to communicate a little more clearly, such as "I don't want to play the baby anymore. I want to be the mommy now."

Encourage your child to share her thoughts and feelings by communicating with words rather than crying, pointing, or hitting to assert herself. If your child tends to just point or cry when she wants something, calmly tell her that you can't understand her and that she should use her words.

Help your child label her feelings by describing them and verbalizing your own feelings, such as "I can see you are sad that you can't finish the puzzle because it's time for bed. But we have a busy day tomorrow and you need to get some rest," or "I'm happy you put your socks and shoes on by yourself." When a conflict comes up, give her the words she can use to explain why she's upset and reinforce that by asking her to repeat them. If a friend takes a toy away, for instance, suggest that your child say, "I was playing with the doll first, and I get angry when you don't share." Not only will she improve her language skills; she'll quickly learn that she's more likely to get what she wants and resolve conflicts with others if she can say what it is that she needs.

Showing Signs of Independence

How often have you heard your child say, "Let me do it!" and "I did it all by myself"? Kids are so proud when they can be self-sufficient, and being able to take care of some of their own needs will be an asset in preschool. It's easy to continue doing everything for your child. But if she doesn't learn to do things for herself, she may feel self-conscious and less capable

> **Real Parents Talk**
>
> I was thrilled the day my three-year-old put his socks and shoes on by himself. Unfortunately, I didn't realize his shoes were on the wrong feet until after he tripped while walking to school.
>
> —Lysa Z., Downers Grove, Illinois

if all the other children, for example, are putting on their own jackets before going outside while she has to wait for help. If you help her learn to put on her own shoes and get dressed, wash her hands, eat by herself (not necessarily neatly!), and put her toys away, you'll be building her confidence and helping her get ready for the world ahead of her.

Sitting Still and Listening

Every preschooler will be expected to participate in group activities like circle time, listening to stories, or singing songs. Many toddlers are very active, and sitting and paying attention for a period of time doesn't come naturally to them—neither does waiting for someone to finish talking before they interrupt. You can help your child develop and practice these skills by going to a toddler class or story time at a library where she can get some experience participating in structured group settings. When she's chatting with you, ask, "Are you done talking?" before responding and encourage her to do the same.

Focusing on a Task for Several Minutes

At preschool, there will be a lot of activities, like puzzles and craft projects, that require kids to focus and work independently from start to finish. Encourage your child to do activities on her own for several minutes at a time. For instance, you can sweep the floor while she colors a coloring page, or you can start fixing dinner while she's working with play dough at the kitchen table. If she doesn't have a naturally long attention span (and most kids don't), start with just a few minutes, and increase that by a few minutes each time. By the age of three, most kids should be able to focus for ten or fifteen minutes on a single activity.

Following Simple Instructions

Your child will be expected to follow simple instructions, like lining up by the door to go outside and obeying basic rules such as putting books back on the bookshelf when she's done. If she doesn't have any rules to follow at home, she will be in for a rude awakening when she starts school and is suddenly expected to do as she's told.

Help your toddler learn to follow directions by first giving one-step directions ("Brush your teeth") and then incorporate a second step ("Brush your teeth and then get in bed") once she's ready. Set a few rules that aren't difficult to follow—"Don't take someone else's toy while they're playing with it" or "Don't color on the walls." If she breaks a rule, dole out a small consequence, such as taking away a coveted toy. Whenever you can, redirect her to a new activity or offer a substitute for a forbidden activity. You might say, "Do you want to read a book instead?" or "You can use the crayons to color on paper, not on the walls." Whenever possible, give her a choice so she'll feel like she has some control. At bedtime, you can say, "It's 7:30—time for bed. You need to put on your pajamas. Do you want to put them on yourself, or do you want me to help you?"

Learning the Beginnings of Self-Control

One of the hardest things for all children to learn is how to think before they act rather than let their emotions take over. However, self-control is also one of the most important skills for success in preschool and later in life. Toddlers are impulsive by nature, so when they want something, they want it now— and they will use crying, screaming, hitting, or even biting to get it. It's hard for young kids to stop and think about the consequences of their behavior before they act on their feelings. You might tell your child to wait in line for her turn to go down the slide at the playground. If she's learning self-control, she'll be able to wait patiently and stop herself from pushing the kids ahead of her, because she knows that misbehaving might cause her to lose her turn altogether. If her block tower falls down, she will understand that inappropriate behavior like crying and throwing a block across the room might lead to negative consequences. Instead, she might decide to start building a new tower or find a new toy to play with instead.

Children (and, let's face it, some adults) are slow to develop this skill, but there are some things you can do to help. Teaching your child the social skills already mentioned in this chapter will get her used to sharing, taking turns, and behaving appropriately. Encouraging her to use words to communicate feelings and resolve problems will help her manage her emotions and show her that talking is more effective than crying or using physical force to assert herself. It's also important to set clear limits around what your child can and can't do and to be consistent by not giving in to her when she has a tantrum or misbehaves.

When your child does have strong emotions, try offering alternative choices; distracting her; or suggesting other ways to deal with her feelings, like sitting in a cozy spot at home, hugging a stuffed animal, or jumping up and down.

Remember to praise your child when she stays calm, waits her turn, and uses her words. Also, set a good example by staying calm and not losing your temper around her. By teaching your child healthy ways to respond to stressful situations, she'll learn to make good decisions on how to act herself.

Don't worry if your toddler isn't Miss Manners by the time she starts preschool. No child wants to share all the time or is well behaved every minute. Children develop at different rates, and preschool will be a time of major social interaction and big leaps forward. Kids also learn by watching the people around them, so be a good role model and act in the way you want your child to act. In time, she will learn to socialize and act appropriately. Meanwhile, be patient and encouraging, and continue to look for opportunities to help your child learn these important social and emotional skills even after preschool begins.

COGNITIVE SKILLS

Kids don't have to start preschool already knowing their ABCs and 123s, but you can teach some basic skills that will give your child a good start once school begins. This kind of learning should occur naturally, through playing and having fun. Flash cards and workbooks aren't necessary. It's just as effective—and a lot more fun—to find learning opportunities in play and everyday life.

General Knowledge

- **Find learning in everyday objects.** You're already surrounded by ways to work in a few academic skills. Point out letters and numbers on streets and buildings. Find different shapes, colors, and sizes in everyday objects. Tell your child the names of everything around her. Incorporate some educational toys that teach the alphabet, numbers, colors, and shapes.
- **Sing songs and nursery rhymes.** Toddlers love songs and nursery rhymes, which help them develop a sense of rhyme and rhythm, as well as their memory of words and sounds. Songs like "Ten Little Monkeys" help teach numbers and counting. All types of storytelling—songs, rhymes,

books—help build your child's imagination and are a fun introduction to the world of literature.

- **Read to your child as often as possible.** Reading aloud helps your child learn vocabulary, start recognizing letters and the sounds they make, and understand that letters make words. Lots of children's books present the alphabet, numbers, colors, and shapes. Reading aloud also develops her listening skills. You may be surprised to hear her repeat a line from a book she heard days ago, or talk about something you read aloud. Whether your child is into trucks or ladybugs, find stories that will hold her interest. And be prepared to read the same books over and over (and over and over and over). You may be bored after the eighteenth reading of *Go, Dog. Go!* but preschoolers won't be. Every time you read it again, your child will get something new from the experience.

- **Teach your child to memorize personal information.** It's a good idea to teach your child to memorize her full name; her parents' full names; her phone number (with area code); and if you can, her address (or at least city). She should also be able to recite them clearly, just in case of an emergency. Make it fun: use a catchy tune, let your child dial the phone number from a different phone, or pretend to be lost in the car and ask for your address.

The following sections share some more ideas to help your child develop language skills and to help you introduce some basic math concepts.

Language and Reading

- **Talk with your toddler every day.** This helps develop language skills and build vocabulary. The more your child gets a chance to talk, the more comfortable she'll be talking with others. Engage her in conversation about everything—what you're doing right now, what she wants to eat, what she likes and dislikes. If she's curious about something, try to answer her questions (if you don't know, say so, and then look for the answer together). If you're reading a book together, talk about the pictures and the story—your child will learn more by conversing than just by listening.
- **Sing the ABC song together.** As you sing the ABCs, point to the letters as you sing them.
- **Teach your child to read her name.** Show her how to recognize the letters in her name and the sounds they make.
- **Use real words.** Most parents naturally speak baby talk to their infants (like *choo-choo* instead of *train*). But as your child gets ready for school, you should gently replace the baby–talk words with the correct names for people, places, and things so that your child can broaden her vocabulary and clearly articulate her needs in class.

Pre-Math Skills

- **Count to ten.** When stacking blocks with your child, count each block as you build a tower. Ask her to count the number of carrots left on her plate. Then after she eats a couple, ask how many are left. Help your child identify numbers by pointing to objects and saying, "Look, that sign has the number seven on it!"

- **Sort blocks and other objects.** Sorting objects by color or arranging spoons and other items from smallest to largest is the base on which your child will build counting, addition, and more advanced math skills. Also, you can explain relative concepts like bigger and smaller, more and less, and taller and shorter.

PHYSICAL SKILLS

Between the ages of three and five, significant development of gross and fine motor skills is taking place. Gross motor skills, such as running, turning, and putting on a coat, use the large muscles of the body and help kids develop coordination and balance. The physical exercise that practicing gross motor skills provides is also vital to children's overall health (experts say preschoolers should get at least an hour of physical activity each day). Fine motor skills, such as drawing and building with blocks, use the small muscles of the hand and fingers. These skills are necessary for manipulating small objects, using eating utensils, and (later on) writing. To help your child develop motor skills, try some of the ideas that follow.

Gross Motor Skills

- **Go to the playground.** Let your child run around, swing on the swings, and climb on the play structure.
- **Turn up the music.** Dance, jump, and march together to the music.

- **Teach new skills.** Show your child how to throw a ball, ride a tricycle, and how to walk up and down stairs using alternating feet.
- **Sing songs or play games.** Use clapping or other actions while singing songs and playing games, like "If You're Happy and You Know It, Clap Your Hands."

Fine Motor Skills

- **Do art projects together.** Art projects let your child practice drawing, coloring, painting, and molding play dough. Teach her to use safety scissors. Art activities help preschoolers develop the hand coordination that they'll need for writing while nurturing creativity and encouraging imagination.
- **Provide toys.** Offer toys such as Legos, puzzles, blocks, and miniature cars.
- **Teach your child self-help skills.** These include how to button and unbutton, zip and unzip, and snap and unsnap clothes; how to eat with a fork and a spoon; and how to drink with a cup.
- **Let your child help cook.** Measuring dry ingredients in a measuring cup, mixing dough, and decorating cookies all help build hand and finger muscles. And your child gets to eat the results!

SEPARATING FROM PARENTS

Kids who are comfortable being apart from their parents for a while will be better prepared to separate from them at preschool. If your toddler hasn't had much experience being away from you, you might want to try practicing separation in the weeks before preschool begins.

Start small—step out of the room for a few minutes while she's playing at home. Next, ask a relative or baby-sitter to watch your child for a few hours or a whole day. You may want to start with brief separations with caregivers she knows well and work your way up to longer time periods with people she's less familiar with. Eventually, you could try taking her to a drop-off toddler class where parents don't sit in. Let your child know what you're doing and tell her about all the fun things she'll be doing while you're gone. Always let your child know that you'll be back, and prove that she can trust what you say by coming back when you said you would.

When your child gets used to the idea that she can safely and happily spend time with another adult, it will be easier for her to separate from you once she begins school. Chapter 14, "Countdown to the First Day of Preschool," will give you some specific tactics you can use as the first day approaches to help your child prepare for being dropped off at school.

POTTY TRAINING

Many preschools require that kids be potty trained before they start school. This can cause many parents stress about meeting the deadline. It's best to start potty training as soon as you see signs that your child is ready. Don't wait for her to ask to use the toilet. If she's uncomfortable when her diaper is wet or soiled, she's ready. (If your child wears disposable diapers, switch to pull-ups—they're less absorbent, so she notices feeling wet.) The longer you wait, the more difficult it will be. You're bound to feel more pressure to accomplish potty training as the start of the school year approaches. It's very important that you don't communicate any of your own feelings of stress to your child. Don't threaten her by saying if she's not potty trained she won't be able to go to school. That means more to you than it does to her at this stage.

You'll want to ease any fears your child might have about going to the bathroom at school. On your visit or on the first day of school, show her where the bathroom is for her classroom. Point out that the toilet and sink are just the right size for kids. Try to give her an opportunity to practice using it. Reassure her that if she has an accident, it's OK, because you've left the teacher an extra set of clothes for her to change into.

Keep in mind that, to a preschool, being potty trained means being completely potty trained. That includes children being able to pull down their own pants, use the toilet, wipe, pull their pants back up, and wash their hands. Don't expect preschool teachers to stand over your child in the bathroom and help her to do any of these things (although schools that allow kids who are not potty trained or are still in the process of learning will usually provide help for kids).

There are lots of books on how to potty train your child, as well as books and videos for children. Even if you don't normally let your child watch television, videos are very helpful for potty training because they show real-life children or appealing characters sitting on the toilet, talking about their concerns, and ultimately being successful. Books and videos make the process fun, which makes kids more interested in participating.

Recommended Books for Parents

- *Toilet Training in Less Than a Day*, by Caleb Azrin
- *Stress-Free Potty Training: A Commonsense Guide to Finding the Right Approach for Your Child*, by Sara Au and Peter L. Stavinoha

Recommended Books for Kids

- *A Potty for Me!* by Karen Katz
- *Going to the Potty*, by Fred Rogers

Recommended Videos for Kids

- *Potty Power—For Boys and Girls* (Consumervision, 2004)
- *Bear in the Big Blue House—Potty Time with Bear* (Walt Disney, 1997)

If the first day of school is approaching quickly and your child is still not potty trained, you have a few options. First, read through one of the books recommended herein for parents to pick up some ideas. If your child will pee in the toilet on her own but poop only in her diaper, take note of when her bowel movements happen. If it's only at night, then she's essentially toilet trained during the school hours, and you can send her to preschool. (But do explain the situation to teachers and let them know that if she does poop during school, you'll come and change her.) The same goes for bed-wetting. If your child can stay dry all day but still needs a pull-up at night, she's trained well enough for preschool.

If your child is almost but not completely potty trained, ask the preschool teacher if she can help. It might be that your child forgets to go when she's busy playing—can the teacher make an effort to remind her often? Schools understand that in the first few weeks, even the most potty trained children can have accidents. There's a good chance that being at school will provide the peer pressure needed. You child might actually be better at using the toilet at school than at home, as the teacher makes it part of the daily routine!

However, if she is really nowhere near being potty trained, ask the teacher if your child can wear a pull-up and then to call you if she soils her pants, so you can bring her home to change clothes. Having to leave preschool early might very well motivate her to learn to use the toilet. Schools vary on how strict their potty-training policies are. Your teacher will let you know if the school doesn't allow pull-ups and may ask that your child not begin school until she's fully trained.

***

Now you know how to help your child be developmentally ready for preschool. In the next chapter, you'll learn how to help your child be personally ready and prepared for the first day of school.

CHAPTER 14

Countdown to the First Day of Preschool

STARTING PRESCHOOL IS A BIG step for a young child, and it can be both exciting and scary at the same time. On one hand, going to nursery school means doing fun activities and becoming a "big kid." On the other hand, it also means being in an unfamiliar setting with a new set of people and rules. This can be especially frightening for children who aren't used to being away from home.

Every child is different, and it's hard to predict exactly how your child will react on the first day. But there are steps you can take to help address his fears and smooth the transition (for you as well as for your child) as much as possible. Let beginning preschool become a process that takes place over a few weeks rather than in one day when everything changes.

DURING THE SUMMER

Stay Organized

You'll be receiving plenty of forms to read and fill out before school starts, like updating your contact information, a list of people who are approved to sign your child in and out, and immunization records from your pediatrician. The school will also let you know whether there will be any opportunities to visit the school or meet other families before the school year begins.

Hold on to your brochures and admissions paperwork on other preschools for now. All that research may come in handy for future reference. You might need it if you have another child who will be entering preschool or decide to send your child to a different school later on.

Review School Policies and Schedule

Many preschools send home a parent handbook full of policies and procedures, staff contact information, the classroom schedule, a list of what to bring on the first day, and more. Learn what the phase-in procedure is and how the teachers will help your child transition to the new classroom. Be sure that you understand the school's policies about meals, drop-off and pickup, discipline, and so on.

Review the school calendar and note when school is closed for holidays, vacations, parent-teacher conferences, and other days so that you can plan ahead for child care. Many families plan vacations to coincide with preschool breaks. You'll also want to figure out drop-off and pickup logistics, such as which parent will drop off on which days, what time class starts, and where you can park. Allow enough time in your schedule, especially for the first few weeks, so that drop-off won't be too rushed.

Make the Most of the Summer

Summer is the time to get your child ready for preschool. If you think it would help your child get comfortable in group settings and used to being away from you, sign him up for a weekly art class or a weeklong day camp. Find out whether a community or parenting center has a class designed to help children get used to being in a preschool environment. If the school has a summer program (and your child meets the age requirement), that can also be a great way to meet future classmates and ease into the preschool environment. Or use this time to just be together as a family or take a family vacation. Before you know it, your child will have a schedule, and it will be harder to do things spontaneously.

THREE TO FOUR WEEKS BEFORE PRESCHOOL STARTS

A few weeks before school starts, you can start familiarizing your child with school by talking about it, visiting the school, and providing books and DVDs about preschool. You don't need to start too soon, as kids this age don't have much sense of time and could either forget about it or wonder what's taking so long.

Talk about School

Talking about preschool ahead of time helps your child to get used to the idea of going to school and to look forward to it. He'll definitely pick up on your attitude, so don't let him see that you're feeling anxious or sad. Be positive when you're talking about school, and your child will be positive, too. Here are some things you can say (enthusiastically!) to your child:

- When you drive past the building from time to time, say, "That's going to be your school!"
- "In preschool, you'll get to draw pictures, play with toys and blocks, and play with other kids. You'll also get to play on the big playground."
- "Miss Gretchen will be your teacher. She's really nice and she'll take care of you and the other kids at school."
- "I'll take you to preschool in the morning, and pick you up after snack time."
- If your child says he's worried about preschool, say, "When I was little, I was afraid to go to preschool, too. But the teacher was really nice, and I made some new friends. So then I wasn't scared anymore."

Also, start using some preschool terms around the house, so when your child draws or plays with play dough, it's art time; when he eats his afternoon graham crackers and juice, it's snack time. Try not to dwell on your child's concerns or keep asking whether he's afraid about preschool. You don't want to put ideas in your child's head or turn a small fear into a large one.

Visit the School
If it's allowed, try to visit the school a few times so your toddler can become familiar with the setting. If possible, introduce him to his new teacher and let him play on the school playground.

Books and Videos
There are some terrific books and videos about starting nursery school that will help your child understand what

happens in the classroom and see how other kids feel about starting school. When toddlers hear or watch a story about a character who feels unsure about starting school and separating from his parents but ultimately learns to enjoy it, that validates their own feelings and helps calm their fears. These stories encourage kids to ask questions about their own school, and give parents an opening to talk through their child's worries.

For parents, a wonderful, comprehensive resource on supporting children throughout their preschool experience, from playdates and discipline to meals and bedtimes, is the book *Practical Wisdom for Parents: Raising Self-Confident Children in the Preschool Years* by Nancy Schulman and Ellen Birnbaum.

Recommended Books

- *The Kissing Hand*, by Audrey Penn
- *My First Day at Nursery School*, by Becky Edwards
- *What to Expect at Preschool*, by Heidi Murkoff
- *I Love You All Day Long*, by Francesca Rusackas

Recommended Videos

- *Buddy Bear in My First Day at Preschool* (Velocity/ Thinkfilm, 2005)
- *Sesame Street—Ready for School!* (Sesame Street, 1990)

Meet Other Families

Get to know some other families from your child's new class. Many preschools have orientations or open houses for parents, teachers, and kids to get to know one another. Some schools provide a class directory with names and contact information. Set up a few playdates so your child can get to know some of his classmates and can walk in on the first day already knowing a few friends.

ONE TO TWO WEEKS BEFORE PRESCHOOL STARTS

The week or two before school starts is the time to get everything your child needs for school. Take some time to acknowledge your feelings about the transition and to be sure that you're as prepared for the first day of school as your child is.

Count the Days

Hang up a calendar and draw a big red circle around the first day of school. Let your child cross out or put a sticker on each day, so he can watch the big day getting closer. Not only will this get him excited about preschool, but also it will keep him from asking, "Am I going to preschool today?" each day.

Establish a New Routine

Kids love routines. They feel comfortable when they know what to expect next and when their day follows a predictable pattern. If your child doesn't have a set routine, start now to slowly create one. Arrange to go to the playground at the same time each day or enroll in a toddler class that meets at a regular time. In preschool, your child will have to follow a schedule and switch gears throughout the day. You can help him get used to making transitions by giving him advance notice when he has to stop doing an activity ("After you ride the tricycle home, it will be time to eat lunch").

> ### Real Parents Talk
>
> I admit it—I let my daughter watch an episode of *Dora the Explorer* before school every day so I can get myself ready for work. The show ends right when we need to leave the house, and she knows that's when it's time to put her jacket and shoes on.
>
> —Jennifer B., Tampa, Florida

If your child stays up late and sleeps late in the morning, start putting him to bed fifteen minutes earlier each day until he can wake up in time to get ready for school. (You might have to adjust your own body clock, too!) Move snack, lunch, and nap times to match the school's schedule. If your child is used to watching television in the morning, try to gradually get him used to not watching it. You don't want to have to drag him away from his favorite show and have him think of school as something negative.

Go on a Shopping Spree

It's time to go shopping for the things your child will need to bring to school. Do you need a blanket for the nap mat? An extra set of clothes to keep in your child's cubby? Preschools typically send a list of supplies, but here are some items that you'll probably need:

- **Backpack.** Find a preschooler-sized backpack that's comfortable and has adjustable shoulder straps so it fits comfortably.

- **Lunch box.** Metal or plastic lunch boxes are sturdy and easy to clean, and insulated lunch bags keep food hot or cold (especially with an ice pack). A thermos keeps soup or pasta warm and milk or other drinks cold. Stock up on food containers of different sizes for everything from sandwiches to fruit. For drinks, use a straw or sippy cup, a thermos, or pack juice boxes. Don't forget kid-sized utensils. Check if the school provides items like milk and utensils so you don't pack anything you don't have to.

- **Bedding.** For nap time, you'll probably need to provide a blanket (and perhaps a sheet and pillow). Store them in a pillowcase to help keep them clean. Some schools allow a small sleeping bag. The school may ask you to bring everything home at the end of each week to be washed.

- **Clothes.** Shopping for new school clothes can be fun, but don't feel like you have to buy your child a new wardrobe. He simply needs comfortable clothes that are OK to get dirty and that he can take off and put on by himself, like elastic-waist pants (especially if he'll be going to the bathroom on his own). For safety, remove any drawstrings from jackets so they don't catch on playground equipment. Sneakers are best for the playground. Some schools don't even allow sandals. You might be asked to pack a change of clothes in case of accidents. Preschool is active and messy—you'll know it was a great day if your child is covered in dirt, paint, and glitter glue.

> **Real Parents Talk**
>
> I use two of his crib blankets as preschool nap blankets and rotate them each week so I don't have to do laundry on the weekends.
>
> —Karin T., San Diego, California

Make back-to-school shopping an occasion. Let your child help pick out his own gear. He'll be so excited to wear his new sneakers. Look how proud he is, wearing his new back-pack all day at home!

Label Everything

Get a permanent marker and put your child's name or initials on everything he'll be bringing into the classroom. That includes clothing (write on the tag or inside the neckline or waistband), blanket, sheet, lunch box, food containers, and so on. You can also buy personalized labels online to iron on or stick on clothing (such as Mabel's Labels at www.mabel.ca).

Plan for Meals

If you'll be packing your child's lunch and/or snack, think about what he'll eat and what's packable. The meal should be nutritious and easy to eat, and it should contain food he likes (not just what you wish he'd eat). Be sure to follow the school's guidelines (e.g., no peanuts, no sweets). Make it fun by letting him help choose the food at the store (which may require some compromising) and letting him help fix the lunch. If kids help make their own meals, they're more likely to eat them. Don't worry if he doesn't finish everything (or anything, some days). As long as he's eating a diet that's balanced over the course of several days, it's fine if he doesn't eat a full meal every time. See the lunch and snack ideas on the next page for some suggestions on what to pack for meals.

Preschool Lunch and Snack Ideas

Sandwiches

Turkey and/or cheese; tuna, chicken, or egg salad; peanut butter and jelly; peanut butter and banana; cream cheese and jelly; tortilla wraps; grilled cheese

Cut into quarters. Instead of bread, try crackers, bagels, English muffins, or pita. Peanut-free alternatives to peanut butter include cashew or almond nut butter, and completely nut-free options include sunflower or soy-nut butter.

Fruits and Vegetables

Fresh fruits such as apples, grapes, oranges, strawberries, blueberries, and bananas; fresh vegetables including carrots, celery sticks, cucumber slices, broccoli, red bell peppers, and snap peas; steamed broccoli, asparagus, and other vegetables

Cut into small bites (including grapes) to prevent choking. To encourage your child to eat veggies, try giving ranch dressing for dipping, adding small, cooked veggies to pasta or rice, placing lettuce and cucumbers or bell peppers in sandwiches, or hiding veggies by pureeing and adding to pasta sauce or muffins.

Hot Food and Leftovers

Pasta and sauce; mac and cheese; pizza; chicken strips; soup with little or no broth; meatloaf; steamed rice or noodles; cut up hot dog with ketchup

Dinner leftovers make quick, easy-to-pack lunches. You can pack the food cold or microwave it in the morning. A thermos will keep food warm until lunchtime.

Snacks

Crackers or pretzels; dried fruit, including raisins; hummus and pita; cubed or string cheese; slices of deli meat; hard-boiled egg; chewy granola bar; applesauce; dry cereal

Dessert

Muffin; canned fruit; pudding; yogurt cup; animal crackers; jello; cookie

Assume your kid will eat dessert first, so keep it small.

Drink Ideas

Water; milk; fruit juice; herbal iced tea

Keep milk cold in a thermos or buy shelf-stable milk that comes in a juice box. Freeze juice boxes overnight so they will be thawed and cold at lunchtime; they will also make a great ice pack for the meal.

Have your child practice eating from his lunch box at home. Let him take everything out by himself, open the packages, drink out of his cup or juice box, eat some food, and then clean up after himself. Although teachers will help, your child will feel confident and independent if he can do it mostly by himself.

Real Parents Talk

I pack fruits and vegetables every day since this is the time when kids can develop a taste for healthy foods. To mix it up, I present them in different ways. I'll make ants on a log (peanut butter with celery and raisins), cut the fruits into fun shapes, or pack low-fat ranch dip with the veggies.

—Sangeeta D., Livingston, New Jersey

STRESS-FREE STRATEGIES
FOR PACKING LUNCH

· Plan and shop for a week's worth of lunches. Stock up on foods you can store, like frozen bagels, deli meat, cheese, peanut butter (if allowed), and baby carrots. Pack perishable fruit like strawberries or grapes early in the week, and oranges, apples, and raisins toward the end.

· Fix lunches the night before, and make use of dinner leftovers. If your kid complains about soggy sandwiches, add lettuce and tomato in the morning. To be really efficient, make a batch of pasta on Sunday and split it into several lunch containers for the week.

· Keep lunch food and containers together in a basket in the cupboard and fridge so you can just bring everything you need out at once.

Learn the Phase-In Plan

Every nursery school has a transition plan, also called the phase-in plan, to help kids ease in to school. Sometimes parents stay in the classroom for a designated amount of time on the first day, then a little less time the second day, and they continue that pattern for the first week. Or the first couple of weeks might be shorter days or fewer days per week.

At some schools, parents stay in the classroom for the first day and participate in a few class activities. Then they sit on the sidelines. When parents think their child is ready, they wait outside the room in the hallway or in a separate room. Some schools host a classroom open house for children and their parents a day or two before school starts but then don't allow parents to linger once class actually begins.

Whatever the plan, let your child know what to expect. Give him an idea of the daily schedule, and talk to him about what will be new and what may be familiar from his current routine. If you think your child will have a hard time at drop-off on the first day, it might be easier if the parent he more easily separates from is the one who brings him to school. During the first couple of weeks, you may want to take a break from other classes or playdates after school so your child can relax after his first days at school. Especially if he's not used to being out of the house and around other kids all day, making sure he isn't overscheduled and giving him some downtime will help smooth the transition.

Visit the Classroom and Meet the Teacher

Be sure to attend the school's classroom open house, if one is offered, before the first day of class. This is a great way for your child to become familiar with the classroom and get to know the teacher while feeling secure that you're nearby. Here are some tips to follow when you're in the classroom with your child:.

- Tell your child the name of his school and teacher.
- Point out activities he'll be doing every day (draw attention to the ones he already likes), and let him explore the classroom and playground.
- Let him choose whether he wants to interact with other kids that day—there will be plenty of time to meet them when school starts.
- Each day leading up to the first day, say something along the lines of "Next week, you'll go to ABC Land Preschool and paint pictures with Miss Gloria."

Be sure to take the time to chat with the teacher yourself, preferably when your child is within earshot. Show your child that you like and trust the teacher, so he can, too. Let the teacher know whether your child has allergies or other medical conditions or is afraid of the dark or thunderstorms. Give her a heads up about any recent events that might affect your child, like the birth of a sibling or a move to a new house. Also let her know what works to comfort your child if he's upset.

Share your child's interests and habits. For instance, "Caleb loves trains and enjoys drawing and reading books about them." Or "Natalie says *wasser* for water, so that may mean she's thirsty." Ask the teacher how she handles separation issues and how you can work together to make the transition as smooth as possible for your child. Because there's a lot to cover, some schools schedule a parent-teacher conference before school starts to discuss these topics.

Don't Feel Bad about Feeling Bad

The beginning of preschool can be a bittersweet time for parents. On the one hand, your baby is growing up and is going to be having a wonderful experience, making new friends, and learning new things. On the other hand, he's not your little baby anymore. Don't be surprised if you find yourself getting emotional about your child going off to nursery school. You're not alone—many parents are going through the same roller coaster of feelings. Talking to your friends in the same situation can be helpful. Reach out to another new parent and go out for lunch or coffee while your kids are at school. After a few weeks, you'll see that your child is happy and thriving at school, and you'll have had time to get used to the idea.

THE DAY BEFORE PRESCHOOL STARTS

It's hard to believe that your child will actually be starting preschool tomorrow! As amazing as that is, it's important to keep the day low-key and relaxing. Here's what you'll need to do the day before the first day of preschool.

Give Your Child a Reminder

In a calm, low-key way, remind your child that preschool starts tomorrow and let him know throughout the day some of the things that he'll be doing there. Then mention it again at bedtime. Say something like, "Tomorrow morning we'll have waffles and juice for breakfast. Then after you brush your teeth and go potty, we'll put on your school clothes and walk to preschool together. Then we'll say hello to Mr. James. I'll give you two hugs and two kisses, and then I'll go out of the classroom. You'll get to stay at preschool and play with new toys, color, and play on the playground. Your friend Noah will be there. While you're at school, I'll be doing work in my office [or whatever you'll be doing]. When you're done, I'll come get you and we'll walk home again."

If your child is worried about school and has questions, listen to his concerns and make positive comments to allay his fears. Don't dismiss feelings by saying things like "Don't be silly!" or "Don't worry, you'll make lots of friends!" Just let your child know that you are confident that everything will go well. You might say, "It might take a little while to make some new friends, but tomorrow you'll get to meet all the other kids. If there's someone you like to play with, we can invite them over for a playdate."

Invent a Good-Bye Ritual

Think of a special good-bye ritual ahead of time and let your child know what it is. It could be as simple as reading two books followed by a hug and a kiss. You could give each other a high five, come up with a secret handshake, or have a silly saying like "See you later, alligator!" Or use the ritual from the book *The Kissing Hand*—kiss his hand three times and ask him to put the kisses in his pocket so he can take them out later in the day.

Get Everything Ready

It's time to pack up all his new gear and everything he'll need for his first day:

- Nap items, like a blanket, sheet, pillow, and stuffed animal (if allowed).
- A change of clothes, including socks and underwear.
- Lunch box—don't forget utensils and a napkin. As a special treat for the first day, you could sneak in a family photo or an easy-to-decipher note (like a drawing of a smiley face or a heart)
- Anything else the school asks you to bring.

Let your child help pick out his outfit for tomorrow (or offer a choice of two outfits), fix his lunch, and pack his things in his backpack. Being involved in the process and having some say in what he will wear and eat will help him feel secure when he's away from you.

- Picking out an outfit—or, offer a choice of two outfits that are acceptable to you
- Fixing lunch or a snack
- Packing supplies in a backpack

A Good Night's Sleep

Be sure your child gets to bed early and has a good night's sleep so he'll be rested and relaxed in the morning. Set your alarm so everyone gets up early enough to eat breakfast together and get out the door on time to arrive at preschool a little early. Allow some time in the morning for him to change his mind about what he wants to eat or wear.

THE FIRST DAY OF PRESCHOOL

The big day is finally here!

Allow Plenty of Time to Get to School

On this day, especially, it's important to allow plenty of time to get ready and get to school. If you've prepared everything the day before, then the morning won't be a mad dash to get out the door. The calmer things are at home, the easier the separation will be when you get to school.

Even if you are running a little late, make sure your child has a good breakfast so he's not hungry and cranky at drop-off. It doesn't have to be a big production. Yogurt, a bran muffin, cereal and milk, or toast with peanut butter plus a piece of fruit and glass of milk are fine.

> ### Real Parents Talk
>
> The first day was so hard—for me. I stood outside the classroom spying through the window for over an hour, sobbing that my baby grew up too fast. She was having so much fun. By the second or third day, I came to my senses.
>
> —Robyn S., West Orange, New Jersey

Go over the day's routine with your child again in the morning and again on the way to school. This will help curb any separation anxiety before it even starts. Resist the urge to bring your camera or camcorder, and focus on easing your child into the preschool classroom. (If you must have a first-day-of-school photo, try to take it at home or outside the classroom.)

Be Positive and Confident

Much of a child's separation anxiety goes back to how his parents are feeling. Show your preschooler you are confident that you're leaving him in a safe place and that you're sure nursery school is going to be great. Let him walk into the classroom on his own—avoid carrying him. Greet the teacher with a smile and in a friendly manner to show that you like and trust her. Even if you're nervous or sad about leaving your child, put on a happy face and pretend you think it's terrific. If your child senses that you're anxious or nervous, he'll be even more scared and clingy.

If parents aren't allowed to stay after class begins, help your child get settled in, put his things away, connect with the teacher, and do your new good-bye ritual before you go. Remember, some tears are to be expected in the beginning, but here are some suggestions for getting through those first few mornings:

- Point out fun activities or other children in the classroom he may remember. Say, "Look at the trains you played with the last time we were here. Remember the track you made? Maybe you can try building another one."
- Don't ask your child for permission to leave—you'll never get it (and it's not his call, anyway).
- Don't sneak away when your child isn't looking. This is very distressing for a child. Let him know you're leaving, and leave.
- Let the teacher get your child's attention and distract him with an activity after you've said good-bye and are ready to go.
- If your child is clinging to you, don't make the teacher have to pull him off your body. That will just make him think teachers are mean and untrustworthy.
- If your child cries, be firm but positive. You could say, "It's time for me to go. I know it's hard, but you'll be OK. Miss Diane will take care of you at school, and I'll be back this afternoon to pick you up."

- Don't drag it out by lingering if your child is crying. Remember, some might take a few minutes longer than others, but all kids stop crying soon after you leave. The longer you stay, the worse it will be.
- If you feel like crying on the first day, save it until you're out the door. Your child could interpret it as "Mommy doesn't think this preschool is a good place, but she's leaving me here anyway."

Yes, it's tough to leave your little one at preschool for the first time, especially if he's having a hard time separating. Remind yourself that your child is in a good place—a place you chose especially for him. It's all right to call the school later on just to see how things are going on the first day.

Guess what? Some kids don't seem to have any separation anxiety. They walk in on the first day like they own the place, head straight for the toys, and barely manage to acknowledge your kiss good-bye. Yes, it's a little heartbreaking, but consider it a blessing!

Be On Time for Pickup

On the first day (and every day), don't be late to pick up your child from school. Let him feel confident that you will always come back when you said you would, and don't make him wonder (even for a moment) whether you're coming.

You may be surprised at how your child greets you at pickup—or doesn't greet you. Just as drop-off is a transition time of day, pickup is a transition, too. Some kids will start crying again when they see you come in the door, so it looks like they've been crying all day. Just ask the teacher. Chances are they've really had a great time. Others run to their parents' arms, full of stories about all the fun things they did at school. Some refuse to leave, insisting that they aren't done playing. (If that happens, be respectful of the teachers' time and calmly but firmly remove your child.)

Give your child some time at home to relax and decompress. He may want some extra individual attention from you, or he may just want to be left alone for a bit. Before going home, however, you might want to celebrate completing the first day of school with a little treat—your child deserves an ice-cream cone, and so do you!

***

Your child isn't a baby anymore—now he's a preschooler! Preschool may start off smoothly; it may be a little rocky. But in a few weeks, that classroom will be full of kids who are having a great time, and your child will be one of them! In the next chapter, you'll learn some tips for helping your child have a great experience in school all year long.

CHAPTER 15

Supporting Your Child throughout Preschool

NOW THAT YOUR CHILD IS in preschool, you can help her get excited about being in the classroom and learning every day. Depending on her temperament, it may take your child two seconds or two months to adjust to the new setting. You can help support her by keeping the lines of communication open with your child and with her teacher and by getting involved in the school community. In this chapter, you'll find tips that will help make the nursery school experience a positive one for your child and your family.

BE PATIENT—THERE'S AN ADJUSTMENT PERIOD

Patience is the key to the first few days. It's natural for kids to take a while to adjust to preschool, so there may be some tears in the meantime. Each child is different. Some will feel comfortable in the classroom from the very beginning; others will take a few days or weeks to acclimate. The usual adjustment period is around three to five weeks of regular attendance.

Don't Assume That Tears Mean Trouble Adjusting

If your child cries every day when you drop her off, talk to the teacher. Ask how long she generally cries after you leave. It may be only a couple of minutes, and then she gets involved in something else. If she cries for long periods of time, she may need some extra help. Work with the teacher to develop a plan to help your child with saying good-bye and becoming more comfortable at school. The teacher may make a special effort to help your child settle in, perhaps giving her a little extra attention or making her feel special by assigning her an important job, like feeding the fish. Some other strategies the teacher may suggest for helping her adjust include the following:

- Keep good-bye time brief and matter of fact (not cold, but not overly lovey-dovey either).
- Let your child bring something from home to hold throughout the day.
- Distract your child each morning with an activity or toy she really likes.
- Have the parent or another relative whom she separates from more easily drop her off.
- If your child cries when you come for pickup, it doesn't mean that she's had a bad day. More likely, she's happy to see you or just gearing up for the transition back to home. Check with the teacher to see how her day was.
- During the adjustment period, make an effort to listen to your child talk about her day and validate feelings about school. If she's having a rough time, it's better to say, "I know you feel preschool is big, new, and a little scary, but every day it will

get a little better, and you'll like it more soon" rather than "Why don't you love preschool? It's so much fun!"

Adjustment Issues

Sometimes kids have a little more difficulty dealing with the changes the start of preschool brings.

Inappropriate Behavior

If the teacher has reported that your child is not adjusting well or having difficulty knowing how to participate in the classroom, she might just need extra help learning appropriate preschool behavior. You can practice things like sitting still in circle time or sharing toys at home and using stuffed animals in the role of the other kids. Before school, remind her of any rules she needs to follow, like hitting is not OK even when we're mad, or to use her words when she wants something instead of crying.

Relapse

Sometimes just as everything appears to be going well for a few weeks, a child will relapse and become clingy at drop-off or announce that she doesn't want to go to school. Your potty-trained preschooler might start having accidents again or wetting the bed. This kind of regressive behavior can be caused by major changes in your preschooler's life or routine—even such seemingly happy changes as a family vacation or a new baby-sitter. Remember, the teacher is your partner. Talk with her about what your child is going through, and work together on strategies that you can use at home and at school to help your child get past any difficulties.

Not the Right Fit

After some observation, you may realize that this particular nursery school is not a good fit for your child after all. It might be too big or too small, too structured or not structured enough, or the teaching approach isn't conducive to your child's learning style. If after discussing the matter with the teacher or director you feel that you have exhausted your options and are certain that your child is not adjusting because the school is not right, you may want to continue looking for other programs that would suit her better.

Contact the nursery schools that accepted or wait-listed your child and possibly some other schools to let them know you're interested in case they have an opening. Also, begin the application process for other schools for the following year. Unless you find an immediate opening in a program you like,

> ### Real Parents Talk
>
> After my son's first six months of school, the head teacher left and the new teacher was not as nurturing and didn't have as much experience teaching preschool. So once we were able to get a spot in another program, we pulled him out.
>
> —Jieun C., New York, New York

your child will likely be placed on waiting lists for some time. You'll need to be patient and continue to follow up with the schools until you get a spot.

Not Ready for Preschool

There are some rare occasions when it turns out a child isn't ready for preschool after all. If she truly cries for long periods every day, acts out or fights with other children, and can't seem to settle into the group's routine after two months or so, it could mean that she's not ready for a classroom environment yet. Children reach developmental milestones at very different rates, and some children may not be ready for school at two or three years of age.

Don't worry. This doesn't mean that your child isn't smart or won't do well in school down the road. You may decide to pull her out of school and wait another year before enrolling again. Check with the school to make sure you will be able to reapply. One year can make a big difference. When your child starts school the following year, you and your child will very likely be glad you decided to wait.

But keep in mind, whether the issue is fit or readiness, pulling your child out of preschool in the middle of the school year should be the last resort. Try everything you can to help her feel comfortable in her new setting, including reducing the number of hours she attends, as most kids do adjust with time. Also, check the school's withdrawal policy to see if you're obligated to pay any tuition for the remainder of the year (see the section "Withdrawal Policy" in chapter 3).

COMMUNICATE WITH YOUR CHILD AND THE TEACHER

Talk with Your Child

Ask your child about preschool every day, so she knows you're interested and to keep up with how she's feeling and what's happening at school. Try to ask open-ended questions to draw your child out. If "How was your day?" doesn't bring about much of a response, try asking more specific, yet open-ended, questions like "What was the favorite thing you did in school today?" or "What book did the teacher read today?" or "What did you eat for snack time?"

For some kids, conversations about their day may go something like this:

"What did you do in school today?"
"Nothing."
"Who did you play with?"
"Nobody."

This is nothing to worry about. If you don't press for answers, the details often come out naturally later on—often when you're driving to and from school or are in the middle of doing something else like eating dinner or at bath time. Just keep your ears open and chat about school when your child is ready.

Show an interest in what goes on at school. If your child brings home art projects, really look at them and talk to your child about them so she knows you're interested. You could say, "Tell me about your picture" (a more effective and encouraging way of stimulating conversation than "What is it?"); ask what her favorite part of the project is; or point out elements you notice, like "You used lots of orange on this page." Hang your child's favorite creations (or yours) on the refrigerator for everyone to see.

If there's going to be a change to the normal routine—like a doctor's appointment or someone else picking up your child—let her know ahead of time. Prepare her for expected changes, too, such as holidays and vacation breaks, or that the school year will end in three weeks.

Talk with the Teacher

Regular communication between parents and teachers is the most important way to bridge the gap between home and preschool. Talking or meeting regularly with the teacher will help you understand your child's progress and exchange information about ways to support her learning and development.

Always inform the teacher or the school of any basic updates: if your child will be absent or if your contact information changes. It's also important for the teacher to know any circumstances that might affect your child's mood or behavior. Let the teacher know if she didn't eat breakfast or didn't sleep well the night before. Be sure the teacher is aware of any major family changes: a new sibling, a move to a new home, a new pet, or even just a houseguest.

Parents and teachers typically communicate in the following ways:

- **Newsletters and notes.** Newsletters let you know about what's going on in the classroom and important upcoming events and dates. Check your child's backpack and cubby for letters from the school (and all that artwork!).
- **Drop-off or pickup conversations.** Although these are hectic times, teachers should have a few minutes to check in with you each day. If you want to speak at length to teachers about your child, bear in mind your teacher's time and whether your child or other children could overhear what's being said.
- **Email and phone.** Email is a quick and effective way for teachers to communicate with parents and for parents to ask questions or let the teacher know about something.

Teachers usually can't answer the phone or respond to email during class time, so if something's urgent, call the school's main phone number.

- **Appointments.** If you have a serious matter that can't be covered in a brief conversation, call the school and ask for an appointment with the teacher or director.
- **Parent-teacher conferences.** These are usually held two to four times during the year for about half an hour. This is when you and the teacher can talk about how your child is doing, whom she plays with, and how she's progressing. You have a chance to voice any concerns and get advice on how to improve the preschool experience.
- **Progress reports.** Many nursery schools send written progress reports assessing your child's social, emotional, academic, and physical skills. Reports are usually given out at the middle of the school year (possibly at a parent-teacher conference) and at the end of the year. Some schools may also send home weekly reports detailing activities and how much your child slept or ate each day.

You should expect to hear from your child's teacher on a regular basis. But if you have any questions or concerns, it's your job to reach out to the teacher. Don't be shy or feel like you shouldn't bother her. Your child is growing and changing so quickly right now—you're bound to have some questions.

Remember to show appreciation for all the things the teacher does. Say thank you or send a note if she does something special for your child or takes extra effort with her. Let the teacher know if your child comes home raving about how fun a class activity was that day or how much you enjoyed reading the class newsletter.

BE AN INVOLVED PARENT

Taking an active role in your child's preschool experience will be valuable to the whole family in many ways. For your child, it shows that you're interested in her and her school. For parents, it's a great way to meet school staff and other parents. This could also be your chance to relive some of life's best moments: story time, field trips, and school carnivals!

What are your talents? What fits your personality? Your schedule? Do you like to work directly with kids or are you better with other adults? Are you more of a behind-the-scenes person who could make cookies for the bake sale, or are you interested in more of a leadership role, like chairing the country fair or the annual fundraising campaign? Does your schedule allow you to be in the classroom regularly? Would it be better for you to serve on a committee that meets in the evening, or would you prefer to volunteer from home or on your computer?

No matter where your interests lie or how busy your schedule, there are so many ways to get involved that you're sure to find the one that suits you best:

- **Attend school functions.** Just going to the many school meetings, potlucks, and presentations lets you meet members of the school community and learn what's going on at the school. Look for social events like family picnics or school-related events like parent-teacher organization meetings.
- **Volunteer in the classroom.** If your school uses classroom

volunteers, you can observe how your child relates to classmates and get a feel for the classroom culture. Teachers appreciate help from parents. You may be welcome to read a story, help out at holiday parties, or chaperone field trips.

- **Join a committee.** Many schools have lots of committees for parents to serve on, such as fundraising, marketing, diversity, parent education, or teacher appreciation.
- **Use your talents.** If you have a talent or special skill, share it with the school! If you're technically inclined, you could help set up the class email list or maintain the school's website. If you play an instrument or sing, volunteer to perform or get a group of parents together to form a band for a school event.

Take advantage of being involved in your child's classroom activities while she's young. The older she gets, the fewer opportunities there'll be (not to mention how much more excited she'll be to have you show up at school now than she will be in middle school!).

Get to Know Other Families

As your child gets acclimated to nursery school (and you get used to this big change, too), try to get to know the families of your child's classmates. Ask your child or the teacher whom your child plays with, and then reach out to the parents to set up playdates. A playdate is a great way for kids to get to know one another better, without all the distractions of the classroom. Playdates are especially important for shy kids or those who have trouble finding their way into a group.

There's a chance you might develop some lifelong friendships of your own. But even if you don't, be friendly with the parents of your child's friends. They can help keep you abreast about what's going on at the school and be a support network of people you can trust to pick up your child if necessary. Doing so also makes all those school events a lot more bearable.

Make an effort to introduce yourself at drop-off or pickup and learn the names of other parents and their kids. If you're a bit shy and find yourself standing on the sidelines when other parents are socializing, look for someone else doing the same thing and go introduce yourself. When you meet other parents, initiate conversation by asking about their kids or for advice you're looking for, whether it's which soccer program is popular among the school families or where the closest playground is.

Take part in social activities, like school picnics, parents-only cocktail parties, or mom's-night-out dinners, even if you don't know anyone yet. The more often you see the other parents, the more you'll get to know them and the more they'll know you. There's also a good chance you'll be spending a lot of time with these families over the next few years, as some if not most of the kids will go to the same elementary school as your child. So invest your time now in getting to know them. After all, you never know if an occasional playdate may turn into a friendship for your child (or you) that will last beyond the preschool years.

> **Real Parents Talk**
>
> I wasn't as active at the preschool as some of the other moms due to my work schedule, but I became friends with some of them by going to as many of the kids' birthday parties as I could.
>
> —Abigail L., Newtown, Pennsylvania

Savor Every Moment

Preschool is fun, busy, stressful, exhausting, and wonderful. It's a very special time in your child's life and one you should cherish. Take plenty of pictures or videos of your child playing with new friends and performing in the winter concert. Help her put together a "My Preschool" scrapbook. And be sure that the crayon drawing "My Family" and the plaster paperweight with a handprint are in a safe place. Your child may have just started preschool, but before you know it you'll be at her high school graduation!

Appendix I

Preschool Comparison Table

Program Attributes	Your Dream Preschool	Preschool #1	Preschool #2	Preschool #3
Affiliations: Public or private, religious, university, YMCA				
Philosophy: Play based, Montessori, Waldorf, Reggio Emilia, academic				
Program type: Co-op, child care center, language immersion				
Age cutoff				
Distance from home				
Weekly schedule(s) available				
Extended care (hours, cost, are elementary school kids allowed?)				

Program Attributes	Your Dream Preschool	Preschool #1	Preschool #2	Preschool #3
Academic-year or year-round program				
Summer program available?				
Cost per month or year (e.g., tuition, extended care, materials fee)				
Financial aid (e.g., sliding scale, loans, scholarship, interest-free payments)				
Single-age or mixed-age classroom				
Number of children in the classroom				
Teacher-student ratio				
Special programs or enrichment classes?				
Teacher credentials and training				
Teacher turnover				
Home-school communication: Parent-teacher conferences, newsletter, email or calls to teacher				
NAEYC accreditation				
School community (parent-teacher organization, social events, diversity)				

Program Attributes	Your Dream Preschool	Preschool #1	Preschool #2	Preschool #3
Preschool only or an ongoing school (through which grade?)				
Elementary schools children attend after preschool				
Potty training requirement				
Separation policy				
Discipline policy				
Includes lunch and/or snacks				
Food policy (e.g., nutritious, no peanuts)				
Parent volunteer requirement				
Classroom drop-in policy				
Sick policy				
Nap policy (length, time)				
Field trips				
Classroom and building (size, well maintained)				
Outdoor area (size, well maintained)				
Safety and security measures in place (sign-in and sign-out, fenced playground)				

Appendix 2

Preschool Profile Form

School name: _____ Phone: _____

Location: _____

Website: _____ Email: _____

Director/admissions director: _____

Age/date cutoff for enrollment: _____ Age range: _____ to _____

No. of spots available: _____ NAEYC-accredited? ❑ Yes ❑ No

Schedule

Availability (days/hours): _____

❑ Year-round   ❑ Academic year (dates: _____) Summer school: ❑ Yes ❑ No

Vacation/holidays/other days school is closed: _____

Extended care (e.g., hours, advance notice required, enrichment classes): _____

_____

Other: _____

Costs

Tuition: $ _____   Meals: $ _____

Extended care: $ _____   Enrichment classes: $ _____

Summer program: $ _____   Late pickup: $ _____

Other fees (e.g., volunteer opt-out): _____

Total cost: $ _____   Sibling discount _____ %

Financial aid (e.g., options, deadlines): _____

Other: _____

Application Process

Application fee: $ _____   Waiting list: ❑ Yes   ❑ No

How to get application: _____

Application deadline: _____   Date applied: _____

Visit dates/times: _____

Can I bring child on tour?   ❑ Required   ❑ Allowed   ❑ Not Allowed

Application form: ❑ No questions   ❑ Short answers only   ❑ Parent statement/essay

Child interview required?   ❑ Playgroup   ❑ Individual   ❑ No

Parent interview required?   ❑ Yes   ❑ No

Student evaluation form required from previous day care/preschool?   ❑ Yes   ❑ No

Other (e.g., additional materials required, criteria for admissions preference): _____

Academic Profile

Grades: ❏ Preschool only   ❏ Day care/preschool   ❏ Ongoing school (through grade: _____)

Educational philosophy/type of program: _____

Classroom: ❏ Single age   ❏ Mixed ages

Teacher-student ratio: _____   No. of teachers per class: _____

No. of children per class: _____   No. of students in preschool: _____

Teacher credentials/training: _____

Special programs/offerings: _____

Home-school communication (e.g., parent-teacher conferences, newsletter): _____

Other (e.g., elementary schools students go to, transitional kindergarten, field trips): _____

Policies

Child must be potty trained?   ❏ Yes   ❏ No

Meals: ❏ Lunch included   ❏ Bring own lunch   ❏ Bring or purchase lunch   ❏ Bring own snack

Food policy: _____

Separation/phase-in policy: _____

Sick policy: _____

Nap policy (e.g., time, length): _____

Discipline policy: _____

Transportation (e.g., driving time, curbside drop-off, parking): _____

Other (e.g., security, parent drop-in policy): _____

School Community

Parent volunteer opportunities/requirements: _____

School community (e.g., parent-teacher organization, social events, diversity): _____

Other: _____

Other Notes

Other (e.g., observations, questions to ask, school officials/parents spoken to): _____

Appendix 3

Tips for Applying to Preschools in New York City

MANHATTAN IS ARGUABLY THE MOST competitive place when it comes to preschool admissions. On average, more than a dozen applicants vie for each spot in approximately two hundred preschools. The city also has its own idiosyncratic way of doing things. If you're looking for preschool here, there are some things you should know:

- **Children enroll early.** It's common to enroll children in preschool when they are two or two and a half years old, and many schools offer toddler programs that start at twelve or eighteen months and automatically admit the children into the preschool program. It's to your advantage to sign your child up for the youngest class, whatever it is, as fewer spots may be available the following year.
- **Apply to more schools.** Because preschool admission is so competitive, parents apply to more schools here than in other parts of the country. It's reasonable to apply to as many as six or ten schools. Like everything else in

Manhattan, application fees (and tuition) are higher than the rest of the country, with some application fees costing up to $150.

- **Getting the application can take work.** Some nursery schools—including the most selective—limit the number of applications they give out. The families are either chosen by lottery (to be clear, this is just for the chance to apply) or by being the first to call and request the application the day after Labor Day. Parents have been known to set up networks of friends, relatives, and co-workers to help them dial and redial to reach their top schools. If you don't get through until the end of the day, you may be told that all the applications are already gone. Many schools, however, will send an application to anyone who requests one. Be sure to find out what system your favorite schools use, and then warm up your dialing finger!

- **Applications first, visit later.** Many schools ask that you submit an application before scheduling a visit. In some instances, applicants need to wait to be invited by the school to come in (and not all families are asked to visit). The visit may just be a visit, or it may be an interview for you and/ or your child, so make sure you know what you're going in for. Also, many schools process applications in the order they're received until the class is filled and then stop. For those schools, apply as soon as you can.

- **Connections matter.** In Manhattan, letters of recommendation from influential people can make a difference. So if you know any current or past parents, board members, prominent alumni, or school staff, ask them for help! A letter or phone call can go a long way, even if your child has already been wait-listed.

- **Tell the director if the school is your first choice.** It used to be common for parents to send a "first choice letter" to their favorite preschool. This practice is no longer encouraged, but it's still a good idea to let one school know it's your first choice by telling the director in person or mentioning it in a thank-you note.

- **No bribing.** Bribes are frowned on in Manhattan, as anywhere else. Schools that do consider your ability to donate will probably make assumptions based on your occupation and employer. If you think it will make a difference to a school, you could ask a reference to hint very subtly about your generosity.

ALTERNATIVES TO PRIVATE PRESCHOOL IN MANHATTAN

- **Preschool alternative programs.** Consider signing your child up at an enrichment center that offers a preschool-like environment, including circle time, free play, snack time, and so on. Places like Kidville (www.kidville.com) and New York Kids Club (www.nykidsclub.com) offer "preschool alternative" programs that any child can join and offer a variety of schedules. Some parents prefer these programs for their flexibility, and others sign up as a backup in case their child doesn't get into a preschool.

- **Public pre-K.** Not all areas of the state of New York offer public preschool, but New York City does. If you don't mind your child waiting until he's four years old to enroll in pre-K, check out the free programs available at the public elementary schools. Admissions are based on a lottery, with priority given to siblings and kids from the neighborhood of a particular school. If you enroll your child in a pre-K program outside of your district, however, it doesn't necessarily guarantee him a spot in that school's kindergarten class the following year. For more information, go to www.insideschools.org or the New York City Department of Education website (http://schools.nyc.gov).

RESOURCES

- *The Manhattan Directory of Private Nursery Schools*, a book by Victoria Goldman, provides extensive information about more than 150 preschools, including tuition, hours, admissions processes, and educational approaches.
- **Parents League (www.parentsleague.org)** is a wonderful organization for New York City parents. It hosts preschool admissions forums and workshops, and the annual Independent School Day preschool fair in the fall. The organization can also tell you about open spots that come up during the year at one of its 300 member schools.
- **Center for Children's Initiatives (www.centerforchildrens initiatives.org)** is the leading child care referral agency. You can call its telephone counselors for information and advice on day cares, toddler programs, preschools, and other child care programs.
- **The Independent Schools Admission Association of Greater New York (www.isaagny.org)** has more than 120 member schools, all of which adhere to the same date each year for notifying parents and to the deadline for families

to accept their offers. Not all New York City preschools are members, so do your research. You can search the database of member schools on the organization's website and read about the admissions process and time line.

- **GoCityKids (www.gocitykids.com).** In addition to the websites mentioned in chapter 6, GoCityKids is another good source for preschool information and parent reviews.
- *Nursery University* **(Docudrama, 2008).** Rent this documentary film, created by Marc H. Simon, for a peek inside the world of Manhattan preschool admissions as you follow five families navigating the system and trying to get their children accepted into nursery school.

About the Author

J ENIFER W ANA IS A MARKETING executive who recently went through the process of researching and applying to preschools for her son. She conceived the idea for this book while doing a pro bono consulting project for GreatSchools, a nonprofit education organization that helps parents find and evaluate preschools and K–12 schools. Jenifer received her bachelor's de-

Photo by Kevin H. Chen

gree from the University of Pennsylvania and an MBA from the Stanford Graduate School of Business. She lives in San Francisco, California, with her husband and two children.